be happy now

Chasing Rainbows

An Enlightening Tale of Hope, Guidance & Self-Love
Through the Eyes of an Earth Angel Dog

Lisa Victoria

Cover Design by 100covers.com
Formatted by formattedbooks.com

Contents

About the Author

Lisa Victoria is an intuitive coach, inspirational speaker, podcaster and author with real life experience.

Through her own personal transformation, Lisa discovered her heart voice and learned how to feel happy now, regardless of external circumstances. Along her way she has also learned how to get excited about the future and move towards this with ease and grace.

Transitioning from the corporate world to help and inspire others in their lives, she lives and breathes and teaches the ethos of trusting the journey, and not chasing the future desired state. Happiness is available in the here and now.

Change is constant and if we learn to embrace the journey's twists and turns, knowing that we are always OK, and that we can choose how we respond to life's events, goals then become exciting, instead of a necessity to fill a cup of happiness, that can already be overflowing.

Lisa now inspires others to find their inner heart voice, happiness and confidence to access the feelings now, and move forwards with a new found inner peace and a zest for life.

When Lisa is not living out her passion serving others, she enjoys creating balance in her life. From being out in nature and the stillness of quietly meditating to re-energise, to being surrounded by friends and family, celebrating life, laughing, chatting and occasionally dancing.

Foreword

Dear reader,
Like some of the themes contained within this beautiful book – namely; synchronicity, intuition and magic; the universe conspired for Lisa and I to meet. A mutual friend said she had a strong feeling Lisa and I should connect. Neither Lisa or I knew why we should meet, yet we sensed with that deep inner-knowing and trusted Karen was right. After many "failed attempts" to talk, as always, divine timing (and not on our own human clock) finally provided the perfect moment.

On speaking, it was one of those conversations where you feel you've just reconnected with a very old friend. It became apparent we'd both navigated incredibly similar journeys - from our health - history, to our relationships, to our work. Our current paths were also very much aligned – both making awareness and expanding consciousness a priority, along with a deep wish to be of service to humanity, in whichever forms it takes us.

It's an honour to know Lisa and a privilege to write a foreword for such a divine soul. She exudes kindness, caring, compassion, clarity and wisdom. 'Be Happy Now' from the Chasing Rainbows series, is a gift to all. I love how encouraging and inspiring this book is. Lisa is one of those rare beings who really walks the walk.

Lisa is an inspiration and her book may just give you that final nudge to take control and make that first step into a brave new world. Through her mission to help others, Lisa's turned her challenges into life lessons and is sharing them with us, so that we too may let our light shine.

Lisa's story is relatable and appealing to everyone, it's not describing something far-fetched. We can all perhaps see aspects of ourselves and our lives in the following story. In addition, Lisa weaves easy, engaging and accessible questions throughout for you to consider. Supporting your own self-discovery and self-enquiry, giving you the tips and tools to begin to see life in a different way. To help you get clearer by focusing on what you really want (and less on what you don't). To explore who you really are and what makes your heart sing.

Lisa reminds us that everything works out in the end, for our highest good. It may restore that optimism in you, so that you too will begin to draw miraculous events into your life. She'll help you reconnect more to your heart (and less to your head!), to follow your intuition, to look out for guiding signs from the universe we often miss, and bring the fun back into your life by making it a game of discovery. To allow you to let go of how to get to the destination, and focus on what you can do here and now.

Be Happy Now is not only a captivating story but also provides tangible guidance to help you make those changes. To bring more awareness into your life, and let the love flow back in. As Lisa says; don't wait, there's never a "good" time to make changes. By picking up this book you're taking a powerful step...

What an earth angel you are Lisa.

With love and gratitude,
Christina
Christina Walker
Ascension Meditation Teacher, Holistic Practitioner & Celebrant

Acknowledgements

Well, where do I start? I am overcome with gratitude for the support I have had in creating this wonderful book and being able to present this to you, the reader.

To all my friends, family and loved ones, you know who you are. By my side every step of the way, encouraging me to keep going, through revisions and what I sometimes referred to as 'blood, sweat and tears'. Yes! You will learn about how I overcame this negative chatter as you venture through the book but it's real and it was part of my journey. This leads me to thanking Richard Wilkins and Elizabeth Ivory for showing me HOW to be my true authentic self, minus the negative chatter. Your continued support is highly valued.

To my wonderful friend and fellow author Michelle Smart for the dog walks and listening to me procrastinate over starting the book. Thank you for guiding me to the wonderful, lovely and amazing editorial coach, Joanne Grant. When Michelle said that manuscripts come alive with revisions and to brace myself, she meant it. That's the moment where I had the 'tears' of overwhelm, but I kept going.

Thank you, Joanne Grant, without you, and your editorial coaching, this book wouldn't have come to life. I thank you, for your guidance, professional wisdom, insight and your belief in me. I loved our sessions and the way you gently shifted me back to the present when on this journey. The words still ringing in my ears 'just start writing'. So, I did!

To my proof-readers - you know who you are. I can't thank you enough for the hours you have spent reviewing this book. English was never my strong point at school (or so I thought and here's *ME* writing a book). In the words of Henry Ford 'Whether you think you can, or you think you can't, you're probably right'.

Thank you, Laurence Davies and Sandra Davies, my amazing parents for the guidance, unconditional love, and supporting me - with my sometimes, seemingly outrageous dreams and ideas, never once did you doubt me. I thank you for being my biggest cheerleaders.

To my wonderful big sister, Tracy Morris. Thank you for always being there for me.

I raise a glass to my Gran 'Ellen' who was an inspiration to me. Told that she would not outlive her 20s and if she did, she was never to attempt to have children due to a health condition. She decided to embrace life, had four children and outlived the doctors, emigrating to heaven at the age of 75.

David, thank you for all of your support, bouncing ideas, proof reading, and everything else you did so I could write.

To Lorna Byrne and Mike Dooley, inspiring me to connect with the angels and the universe who in turn presented the idea of this book into the forefront of my mind. That one fateful event in London, created this very book.

I am deeply humbled by the opportunity that John Biethan from the Alternative Health Tools' podcast gave me. I only went to a networking event in California to make friends and that's where we met. He had faith in me and created space for me to be a part of the Alternative Health Tools' family, which I continue to be eternally grateful for.

To my wonderful cousin and her husband. Samantha and Gary Fletcher for welcoming me into their home. Creating memories to treasure in California and helping bring some of the scenes in this book to life. Thank you for your infectious, fun-loving energy. I'll be back!

Christina Walker, another beautiful earth angel, ascension teacher and celebrant. Thank you for your words of encouragement and input to this book, particularly the foreword.

Thank you, Helen Liang, for your hours and hours of copy editing. You are an absolute legend and amazing at what you do.

Almost lastly and not least, my four-legged earth angel Lord Louie. I am super grateful for you 'being' in my life and making this book possible. Without you and the precious memories we have shared, there would be no story to tell.

Lastly and not least of all, you wonderful people out there, reading this book. I thank you for taking this opportunity to read our book and reflect. Whatever you have going on in life, I hope this book serves as a reminder or inspiration to live 'deliberately'. Thank you for enjoying this journey with us.

Preface

Dear Reader,

The night before I was due to see two inspirational speakers in London, I sat and watched a YouTube video of them to learn more about their work. In that video, they simply invited me to complete an exercise. This was to take a piece of paper and pen and to 'ask your guardian angel for guidance on what you needed to know'.

At 11pm that evening I did just that. It was at this moment that 'Be Happy Now - Chasing Rainbows' the series was born, the inspiration and the ideas just flowed. I looked down at the piece of paper 10 minutes later and I had an outline for this very book. So, what did I do next? Ignore the calling, or just take the task in hand and start writing? Given that you're now reading this book, you'll know that I decided to take action. Overcoming my fear of never having written a book before, I said yes to the whisper from the angels and embraced the journey that was before me.

As life would have it, once I succumbed to the task in hand and refused to be held back by my own limiting beliefs, the right people presented in my life at exactly the right time. My wonderful book coach for one. Thank you, Joanne Grant.

As a coach, speaker and author, I have spent the last decade and more, inspiring people to create change and live the happiest, contented, most fulfilling life they deserve. Probably most importantly of all, giving people hope to know that there is a different way.

The journey that led me here…

After battling with 'people pleasing', that is to say constantly living my life to please others or living in fear of what people would think of me, I connected with my inner heart voice, my inner guidance and I trusted the process. I put my head above the parapet and made the commitment to myself that it was my life and I would choose to live it in the way that it helped me to be the happiest, most fulfilled version of me.

It took inner strength, confidence and resilience. I knew that the only way to be truly happy was to be 'me'. The unique version of me. No longer trying to fit in, people please, run myself into the ground trying to keep everyone happy and forgetting to include myself in the equation. I went on to discover my unique gifts, meet wonderful people along the way, develop amazing connections with 'like-hearted' people, and learn skills I would never have learned before. All because I listened to my heart, my soul, my gut instinct and trusted that if I did this, I couldn't go far wrong.

Early on in my journey I discovered energy healing and trained to become a Reiki Practitioner, to help heal myself and others. I said 'yes' to connecting with angels and universal energy. Being open to opportunities and realising that life is a journey, and that all I needed to do was follow what was put in front of me, without judgement, allowed me to trust the process. I learnt how to overcome negative beliefs that were holding me back from achieving my true potential and happiness.

As I said 'yes' to life and opportunity, my experiences kept on unfolding. I realised that I was not only enjoying my journey but I was quickly becoming a respected coach, speaker and now author, and that this allowed me to be able to help others on their journeys too. What I discovered was that life has a habit of presenting challenges, lessons, and teachers to us at just the right time; keeping us growing, evolving and questioning whether we are truly living the life we deserve.

Succumbing to the flow of life and learning how to embrace this wonderful journey, I am pleased to present you with, 'Be Happy Now', from the Chasing Rainbows series. This book is partly fictional but also based partly on experiences and lessons I've learnt throughout my life. I want to share these with you, as the reader, to give you hope, fire in your belly and get you out of your comfort zone. Take action and embrace life for what it is and what YOU truly deserve.

With love from my heart and magical universal energy.

Lisa Victoria

Introduction

Lisa Victoria & the angels

I was guided to write this book through the eyes of my handsomely intuitive, four-legged earth angel, Lord Louie. I would refer to him as my dog, but he prefers earth angel.

Given that Lord Louie is the main narrator in this book, let me share with you how I attracted Louie into my life by trusting my instinct and acting on it.

On holiday a few years ago with my parents, a deep knowing came to me that I wanted a companion. Common sense told me I shouldn't get a dog because of the commitment involved and all other ludicrous reasons as to why it wasn't a good idea. But I chose to follow my heart, not my head and made the commitment to myself and my future companion.

My whole world changed three weeks later when I met Lord Louie.

Have you ever heard people say 'the dog picked me'? Well yes, that's exactly how it happened. I picked up many different pups from his litter and as I held them in my arms I asked for a sign as to the right match for both me and my new companion. As he nuzzled his chin into my knitted V-neck jumper and fell fast asleep, that was my sign. It had to be Louie! A couple of weeks later I went to collect him to bring him home and we have been inseparable ever since.

He brings me joy, love and happiness. He has taught me how to live more in the moment; how to appreciate the small things in life and how to love unconditionally. He's my world, and every day I practice gratitude for having this intuitive, clever, funny soul in my life. He's my 'earth angel'.

Louie will be sharing many of the lessons with you as we journey through the book. Including:

How to:
be happy now;
find hope, guidance & self-love;
feel content;
feel inspired;
love yourself again;
turn dreams into reality;
connect with your soul, your passion, and universal energy
to get back into flow and allow life to be meaningful;
trust in divine guidance and let go of
trying to control everything.

My wish is to inspire you, to know how amazing and special you are, and what you are truly capable of achieving when you believe in yourself; having the confidence to say 'yes' to opportunities, and knowing how to access the intuition and start living deliberately and with 'purpose'.

Lord Louie

Huh hum, before we start, move over mum. As the main narrator. I'd like to introduce myself.

I'm a black and tan cocker spaniel with the longest eyelashes in the world - yes, most women are envious, but they help me look even cuter when I want something! As an intuitive coach in disguise as an earth angel, I observe and intuitively know more than you humans think I do about life and happiness. Most importantly, I feel the connection to energy more than you sometimes do. Have you ever walked into a room and you just 'know' there is something wrong or something right? That's what I'm referring to, it's an energy thing.

I feel passionately about you humans living your best lives and sadly I witness you being stressed, unhappy and waiting for happiness more often than when you live in the moment and embrace your life and the journey itself.

My aim throughout this book is to give you a different perspective on life, and along with mum's knowledge and experiences I will observe, feedback, and present Lord Louie's lessons throughout. I invite you to embrace the lessons at the end of each chapter, taking time to reflect on the questions and discover your uniqueness.

We hope you enjoy reading this book as much as we enjoyed writing it.

With love from,
Lisa Victoria, Lord Louie, and the angels.

Be Happy Now - Chasing Rainbows

It's time to let go
To be free, and just know
When life seems stagnant
Get back into flow

Twists and turns
Or so they may seem
Supporting and guiding you
Soon, to be on full beam

Trust in you
Immerse yourself now
In this book
Learn more on the 'how'

How life should be
No matter what we see
Just plant a little seedling
Witness patiently

Whisper your desire
To the universe that knows
The quickest way to get you there
Accept the way it flows

The answer, not always obvious
Don't question if it's working
Just trust in the magic
Your heart's desires, let them sing

Keep focused on the outcome
Don't try to make sense of it all
You may think it's not possible
For the universe, no order too tall

Timescales out of the window
In the universe, please trust
Plant the seed and feel it
Take a step, it's a must

For what we think we want
And indeed, when we want it by
With our free will decisions
The universe can but try

Make decisions through love not fear
Even if you can't fathom now
Let the universe make the plan
Presenting options for the 'how'

It may not be part of your plan
Surrender and let go
The universe has heard your heart's whisper
Trust and let it flow

Before you get into the flow of the book, we invite you to download your complimentary workbook with Lord Louie's questions from the end of each chapter, to support your own self-discovery as you go. There really is huge value in writing things down as opposed to just 'thinking' it through.

You can get your workbook here:
heartvoice.co.uk/behappynow

chapter 1

RESILIENCE

'the ability of people or things to recover quickly after
something unpleasant, such as shock, injury, etc.'

Oxford English Dictionary

The calm before the storm

Our life as we knew it was, umm, well…how can I put it gently? It was stagnant and it was hard work. It was unsynchronised, stressful and boring. There, I said it. Might as well start as I mean to go on.

Mum or Ellen as she's known to others, often stayed in her comfort zone, afraid of change. Her partner was ticking a box, pleasant chap, kind, or so she thought. Her job was ticking a box, paid the bills, offered security or so she thought! She secretly wished she could help others and occasionally dreamed about being a coach, but she'd 'made her bed' as an accountant so she was lying in it. Her personal life was, well, uneventful. She lived for the weekends, working hard all week in a 9-5 job, studying in the evenings for her professional exams and then if she had any energy left at the weekend, then maybe she would do something fun.

I refer to her life then as 'stagnant'. She was merrily bobbing along. There was no spark or spontaneity. To be frank, it was like Groundhog Day. Temporarily, she would get excited about the end being in sight with her exams and she would often say, 'I'll be happy when I've finished this exam, I can have a break before studying for the next one.' Well, shoot me now I thought. If you have to wait to be happy all the time, then what's the point?

I could see so much more potential within her and gifts she was yet to discover. I respected her journey and walked by her side. This was my job as an 'earth angel', to guide her on her journey. Mum naively thought life would be a 'happy ever after' but, she was soon to learn that life is what we choose it to be. We create our own reality and indeed happiness **is** along the journey, not just at a destination.

Granted, she had a lot going on, full time working as a professional accountant, part time studying at weekends and evenings, as well as learning to Rock & Roll dance. She loved the idea of the petticoats and that was her escapism. She always felt guilty when she went out to dance, but it was her release. Her time. I wished she wouldn't feel guilty and just allowed herself that enjoyment. Sometimes I stayed in with Jim (her boyfriend) and other times I went to Lola's. Lola is mum's best friend, and mum to my best four-legged friend, Bella.

Mum looked beautiful when she went out. This was the time when I glimpsed her light inside, sparking up her creative side but sadly it didn't last; it was momentary, only when she was going out dancing. She had a lot to learn about life, what made her heart sing and how she could weave more of this joy into her life by becoming aligned with her heart.

I know that most humans feel like this at some time or another, it's so easy to feel guilty when you want to do something for yourself and it's easy to fall into the trap of feeling that perhaps 'you are selfish and not doing what is expected of you'. Do you feel that way? Sometimes it's good to take a step back and consider this and if you do feel like this, you shouldn't. It's your time to recharge!

The brewing storm

I remember it clearly; it was a Saturday evening and mum returned home early from dancing. I had been home with Jim. She'd been with him a fair while, the relationship was steady, but I knew he wasn't right for her. She deserved better, they weren't compatible and she was settling. I think deep down she knew it too, but she was scared of being alone. Instead, she put up with having to do all the chores, she forgot to value her happiness and it broke my heart to watch. Have you ever experienced that feeling or been in that position?

As she walked through the door and caught Jim sitting on the sofa with the girl from next door, they jumped apart and instantly she knew. Mum's body language changed; her shoulders slumped. I could see her heart start to pound and tears gently creeping from the corners of her eyes. She ran upstairs, I was on her heels. I knew she was going to need some unconditional love.

Unfortunately, this rendezvous with the neighbour had been happening every week while she was out. Shame I couldn't talk and tell her what a twit he was. However, this is the magic of everyone's journey. Often, even when loved ones give you advice, you fail to act on it until you are ready. She'd known that things weren't right. But, if she wasn't going to take action, then the universe would be sure to come and clout her around the head and force her hand. That night, it did just that. Her dance had finished early due to a power cut. She didn't know it at the time, but it was the first blessing in disguise.

I witness too often you humans ignoring the whispers from the universe and then waiting until it is so bad before you take action.

The next day, after a night in the spare room, and with eyes red raw, she looked numb, scared and was packing our bags to leave. We left without a word. An eerie silence. That was one thing about mum, she hated conflict and couldn't see the point in expending energy on something that wasn't salvageable. With nowhere else to go, we moved in with Lola and Bella. Every cloud has a silver lining, and this was the first one.

"What happened?" asked Lola. Mum went on to explain the story. Lola on the other hand wasn't quite as calm as mum, and in her protective friend mode wanted to go around and punch Jim's lights out. Thankfully, she didn't and they drank wine that night instead! You humans drink when you've something to celebrate and drink to drown your sorrows. Is there any time you don't drink?! She was yet to learn that everything in life happens for a reason, to realign you if you're not in flow. Flow being at the core of your soul, your heart's desires, the path you truly deserve to walk, effortless and with ease when everything is aligned inside of you, no turmoil or conflict.

Skipping a beat

Several weeks later, life was ticking by. I still got the impression that mum felt like she was in a holding pattern and that this time, she would be happy when she had gotten her next lot of exams out of the way. She was spending all her free time studying which meant I got to hang out with Bella and Lola. Needs must, so I didn't mind.

On one particular day a blood curdling scream came from mum upstairs. "Lola!" What? Something must be wrong, that doesn't sound like mum. All three of us rushed up the stairs to investigate.

"Call an ambulance, I think I'm having a heart attack," cried mum.

Through all the panic and chaos that ensued over the next hour, I knew that mum was going to be OK. As Lola closed the front door after watching the ambulance drive off with mum, we all retreated to the living room and curled up on the sofa. It was unsettling for everyone and of course I missed her, but I trusted she was in safe hands and would be okay.

It had been a long day and after a fairly disturbed night, Lola had been tossing and turning, worried no doubt. The phone rang. It was the hospital. Mum was being discharged but was undergoing formal investigations for a heart arrhythmia. "This can't be possible, she's only young," said Lola. "Yes, I'll come and collect her."

Around an hour later, they returned home, looking exhausted. Thank goodness for good friends who are there in your hour of need! As mum went upstairs to get showered and changed, I was on her heels again. I watched her undress to discover she was wired up to a heart monitor. As she looked down at it, you could see she was worried and scared about what this could mean for her future. I had an inkling it was just stress, but I'm no doctor, just her coach and her earth angel. I'd have to leave that one to her consultant to confirm.

Home is where the heart is

After these events, and as grateful as mum was to Lola, she decided that it was time to look for a home of our own. As we scoured the streets of Towcester, the cutest little market town near Silverstone, we viewed many houses and found a suitable home which mum put an offer on. Dismayed that the offer had been rejected, mum couldn't understand why this was happening. She felt frustrated and out of control, like life wasn't fair. Sometimes you just have to let life flow. It obviously wasn't meant to be, but mum was trying to force it. One day she would learn that life sometimes has bigger and better things for you humans that you just haven't discovered yet.

After a period of time where she had felt despondent, we finally discovered our perfect home. It was an energy thing. This one just felt 'right' and it was on Caernarvon Close too, much better than the previous house she had put an offer on. I knew this resonated so much with mum, she was starting to experience the synchronicity of life and be guided by her heart. Mum grew up in Wales, so the fact that the road was named after a Welsh town further embedded the feeling in her heart and she decided to put in an offer.

That evening she explained to Lola her excitement but also her fear of being solely responsible for the mortgage. What if she couldn't manage, what happened if she couldn't afford it? Rather than being excited, she was a little miss worry pants. She hadn't even signed the papers yet! It wasn't even as if it was a rushed decision. The accountant in her had done her maths, so what was she worried about? Her focus was on everything that could go wrong rather than what could go right. Do you ever do this?

Several days later the estate agent called with the news that her offer had been accepted. Mum went through an array of emotions, jumping around the living room, from excitement to fear and worry, and back to joy. It's fascinating that even when you humans get some great news to celebrate, you often experience negative emotions creeping in, and with no front door to securely lock them out, your moment of unadulterated happiness is temporarily interrupted.

Secure & steady

Later that week, mum was working from home. She was still studying towards her exam and still had to wear the heart monitor for a few more days. A call came in from her boss asking her to go into the office the next day. He was a nice chap, close to retirement, who ran a privately owned firm with only a few employees.

"Of course, I can have Louie for the day," said Lola. "You go and sort out whatever you need to in the office."

The next morning mum climbed into her blue Ford Focus and set off for work. Isn't life an adventure? Twists and turns! I know mum was finding it tough. She likes to feel in control and plan everything. That's why she was so unsettled at this point, there was a lot of change. With the relationship break up, new living environment, and an expensive purchase on the horizon, she was just grateful for her steady job. I knew this because she'd mentioned it to Lola just as she was leaving that morning. At least something in her life was providing stability, even if it wasn't making her heart sing.

Later that evening as the Ford Focus pulled up on the drive, I ran excitedly to the door to greet mum. If nothing else, surely, I'd be able to welcome her home and cheer her up after a dull day of accounting. Sorry to all the accountants out there, but mum was a square peg in a round hole and to her, it was dull. It doesn't matter what makes you shine, but for mum this just wasn't her bag. She was good at it because she was diligent, stubborn and wanted to prove she could be a professional. Pfft! She was born to have a good time, not prove that she was clever, who cared anyway? Have you ever felt or are you feeling like you're a square peg in a round hole? If so, is this good enough?

Mum walked through the door with the most vacant look on her face, tears in the corner of her eyes, just like the moment she realised Jim was cheating on her. What on earth has happened now? She had only been gone a day.

"Ellen, what on earth?" said Lola. I did a double take. Was Lola reading my mind? "Come and sit down, you look like you've seen a ghost. Is it your heart? Are you OK?"

"No, it's my job. My boss is having to re-think the business. Clients are dropping off and he can't afford to keep as many staff. There may be redundancies. I don't think I can take it anymore. The house on Caernarvon Close may not happen now. What's the point in even doing my exams? Everything is crumbling around me."

I sat and cuddled mum, there was nothing else to do. Only she could find the inner strength and resilience to get through this. I believed in her, I just wished she would too. The point was, nothing had happened yet, and she was thinking about the worst-case scenario.

We all jumped as her mobile chimed, it was Nana and Gramps from Wales. Universal timing, maybe they would provide the next clue?

As she hung up, she announced that she and I were going to Wales the following weekend for a little respite, to a little cottage, Tyddyn Bach, where my grandparents lived.

Brace yourself

After a relaxing weekend in Wales, we'd been thoroughly spoiled and mum had brought Nana and Gramps up to speed on our adventures, or as mum referred to it, dramas. Life was unfolding. I knew it was for the better, but mum couldn't see this yet. We set off for home, to Lola's. It was our home for now.

We were several hours into the journey and I had been dozing on and off. I was strapped into the back seat in my 'bra' (well, it's a harness but it looks like a bra, doesn't give me much street cred but it keeps me safe,) when from the front of the car came another blood curdling scream.

"Louie! Hold on tight!" Mum's voice was desperate. Please, please, please help!"

As I sat up and looked through the front window, I could see the cars stacking up in front of us. Mum was pressing the brake but nothing, just nothing, and our car was still hurtling at 80 miles per hour towards the back of the stationary traffic.

With some quick-thinking mum started to force the car down the gears in an attempt to slow our speed. Her brake line pipe had failed and it was the final straw. Or was it?

Come on angels, please do something I thought. I don't think mum can take much more. Then, as if by magic, the traffic cleared and the motorway ahead was eerily empty. To this day I don't know where the traffic went but once again, someone was looking after us.

As we came to a safe stop on the hard shoulder, I could see tears streaming down her face in the rear-view mirror, her gaze looking empty and numb.

There was nothing I could do in that moment, I'd lost her to sadness, to fear, and I could see that she felt her life was crumbling around her even more than ever.

I knew this was the universe waking her up, realigning her and inviting her back into flow. The gentle whispers had been present, but she ignored them and the angels were not going to let her get away with a mediocre life. If only she could see that this was the beginning.

As we were rescued and arrived back at Lola's, mum was like a rag doll, with no energy, it was like life had been knocked out of her. She had 'gone' completely, I could no longer see any sparkle. She'd even lost her love for dancing, the one thing that helped her to come alive.

A week of success

As the next week unfolded, mum returned to the hospital I wasn't allowed to go to. Lola went instead. Mum was in a blind panic and Lola tried to calm her down, reassure her that no matter what the outcome was, she could handle it and that there would be a way that things would work out. Of course, mum couldn't hear these wise words and until she decided to change, she wouldn't be able to control that inner dialogue. You humans are good at offering others advice on how to control your thoughts and emotions, yet you seldom give yourself the same advice from a place of clarity and kindness.

When they returned from the hospital, I found out that I had been right all along. The doctor had confirmed that mum's symptoms were due to stress and that it wasn't a malfunction with her heart, it had been caused by anxiety and panic attacks. The body is clever in giving you signs if you're misaligned and again, unfortunately she wasn't tuned in enough to spot them. A little weight had been lifted from mum and she realised she had worried for nothing. One day she would learn to trust. I knew she was on her journey and that the right teachers would present themselves to her at the right time. Now, after these recent wake up calls, something had to change.

Mum sat her exams that week and wasn't confident in her performance. But now that they were over, at least she could relax (her words)! Have you ever considered learning the art of relaxing 'in the now', instead of waiting for something to be over? Mum hadn't yet.

Throughout all of these events, mum had shown that she was more resilient than she thought. You humans are. I just wish you could sometimes see it for yourselves. When forced into situations, you step up, grow, and learn to survive. So, my question to you would be, why don't you do this with your dreams?

The lesson mum needed to learn here is that there are always two options. The first is to wallow in self-pity and think it's everyone else's fault and completely out of your control; or the second is to chalk it down to experience, suck out the learnings and move on with the wonderful gift of growth.

LORD LOUIE'S LESSONS

What are you fearful of? Not having enough money, being alone, or are you scared of making changes in your life? Whatever it is, please don't settle. Just like mum, you are always more resilient than you think. It could be your career, your relationship, your hobbies or your 'self-care' regime. No matter how big or small, there are always eloquent whispers on how to live a more fulfilled life. Mum just experienced a huge shift all at once. Perhaps, had she listened earlier and not acted like an Ostrich, burying her head in the sand, she would have dealt with them in a more measured way. But no, she doesn't do anything by half.

Here are our first lessons from the book. Please take time to reflect and see what you discover.

1. Is your life stagnant? Be honest with yourself! You don't need major shifts, but if your heart knows different from your head, then why aren't you listening to it?
2. Reflect on times in your life when you have undergone transformation. Are these examples of your resilience, and what did it show you? Can you translate that into your present moment?
3. What gentle whispers have you been receiving recently? If you can't think, take some time to reflect. Is everything synchronised in your life, or are you being guided gently back towards your flow?

4. What are you going to do about this? Go on, I dare you to dream. Grab a pen and paper and write down all the whispers you've been receiving, and what steps you can take to move back towards the flow.

Resilience

Has life thrown you curveballs?
Caught you off guard?
Changed your destiny?
Or handed you a red card?

You're stronger than you think
You've perhaps learned something new
About the person inside
A person you never really knew

Your resilience is a gift
To help you get through
Times that are tough
To a life that feels new

Trust in yourself
And your inner resilience
Step out of your comfort zone
And into your brilliance

Connect with your dreams
Don't settle for less
Be grateful for the learnings
For those, you must bless

You are more resilient than you think
More resilient than you'll ever know
Why not put it to the test
Step out of fear, and into flow

chapter 2

ELOQUENCE

'Quality of delivering a clear strong message'

Cambridge Dictionary

A strong message from the angels and the universe

Boy, didn't the angels and the universe deliver a strong message! They are constantly delivering messages, but sometimes you humans bury your heads and ignore them, coming up with excuses as to why now is not a good time. Perhaps this is because you constantly feel that there is a lack of choice but really, is there ever a good time? Alternatively, you wait until the universe really has to swipe the rug from underneath your feet, just to get you to listen and surrender.

About a week after being rescued by the angels on the motorway, (*by the way, they are always listening, all you need to do is ask for help,*) we were walking down a cobbled little back street in Towcester with Lola and Bella.

Mum still hadn't gotten over the recent events and all she wanted to do was to relive them and question whether she'd done the right thing. These thoughts were all tumbling out of her mouth so fast, I could see Lola trying really hard to keep up.

"Maybe I should've stayed with Jim? Who am I to think the 'perfect' man exists? If I'd stayed then I wouldn't have put an offer in on a house whilst being put at risk of redundancy, and perhaps this whole health scare thing would never have happened?"

We were suddenly halted in our tracks by a door opening to the left. The bell's 'ding-a-ling' caught mum's attention as a lady almost bumped into her leaving the 'Cosmic Whispers' holistic health shop. At least that stopped her in her tracks and it stopped her questioning herself.

The bell reminded me of the scene in 'It's a Wonderful Life', where they say, 'every time a bell rings, an angel gets its wings'. This was definitely a clear sign from the angels, gently calling for a change in direction of mum's thoughts.

The lady looked angelic herself, and I could tell mum was thinking just this. She was stunned into silence, as if her life was slowing down and she was catching her breath. The lady had a coloured glow around her, it's called an aura, and I could tell mum was seeing this for the first time. It was almost as if she had felt this lady's energy. Mum's shoulders softened and she breathed a quiet sigh. I'm not sure she even noticed her physiology melt at that moment.

As the lady smiled and turned to pat me, mum turned to Lola and whispered, "Lola, I think I'm having after effects from the stress. I just saw a colourful glow around that lady. Don't tell anyone, else they might lock me up. I'm losing it".

Through happiness, I smiled internally. She's not losing it - she's gaining it - her consciousness that is.

Mum quickly turned, cheeks flushed, checking that the lady hadn't heard her. As she did, she caught a glance of a beautiful angel figurine in the window, with crystals embedded up and down its body and different colours for each of the energy points, known as the chakras. Of course, mum didn't know what a chakra was yet, but she would soon learn how chakras in our body are like little wheels that need to be in balance to keep the universal flow of energy, keeping you humans healthy and happy. More than anything mum was definitely in need of some re-balancing.

"What is Reiki?" Mum asked softly, as her eye caught the sign in the window.

The serene looking lady went on to explain that it's a practice that focuses on relaxing and rebalancing the body's energy flow and that the term means 'universal life energy'. Mum looked at Lola perplexed. She hadn't heard of this practice before, but I could see she was drawn to the idea of it.

"I've had a cancellation this afternoon if you'd like to experience it?" said the lady.

Mum hesitated, "Umm, yeah. I just don't know about this afternoon, maybe some other time? I've got Louie." As she turned to look at me for a 'get out of this situation' excuse.

"It's OK. Well behaved earth angels are allowed to accompany you, it's therapeutic." said the lady smiling.

And there you have it, eloquently whispered from the universe - mum's next venture. As I've been saying, sometimes you humans just have to accept what's in front of you, go with the flow and experience life. What's the worst that could happen?

Parallel universes

As we entered Cosmic Whispers that afternoon, I knew mum was in for a treat. She looked a little nervous, unsure what to expect and worlds away from her accountancy life. I wish she could see what I could see, but instead, she hid, timid and low in self-belief. She questioned everything including herself, always looking for reassurance.

The same lady greeted us and was so calm and serene, she almost floated across the floor to welcome us.

"Follow me." she said as she wound her way up some crooked stairs. The building must have been 300 years old, full of character with beams and uneven walls, salt lamps with their warm orange glow dotted around. There was such a tranquil energy and I could see mum starting to succumb to this wonderful calming environment. Just what the doctor ordered, I thought. Now this is more like it, this is how life is supposed to be. Mum always feels guilty about treating herself, always too much to do on her list, and as an accountant doesn't want to 'waste' money on pampering too often. After all, she needs to save for a rainy day. Yawn! I'm so pleased she was guided by the angels on this one, it did her good.

As we entered the room, there was a diffuser going with beautiful smells of lavender and wild orange, very calming for the mind and the body. It was clear that the lady had invested in quality essential oils and knowing that plant extracts are immensely supportive in healing the mind and the body, I was relieved.

The room was warm and cosy with blankets on the massage bed, sorry I should say Reiki table, all ready for mum to indulge and relax.

As I sat and watched mum laying on the table, the lady placed her hands over mum's body. She started hovering her hands over her head, eyes, throat, then down to her heart space, before continuing over her abdomen and right down to her feet. She remained over her heart space for a while, as if she knew there was energy to be cleared and that a block was present.

Mum looked so relaxed. It was such a pleasant experience for us all. Let me paint a fuller picture for you. She was fully clothed in case any of you are wondering what this Reiki is all about. It's not a massage. It's a practice whereby a fully qualified and trained practitioner will deliver a form of healing by placing their hands over your body. It's a practice designed to relax and balance your energy to support healing.

As the hour drew to a close the lady invited mum's consciousness back into the room. She looked sleepy and calm but was smiling. The lady asked how she felt and she just smiled and said, "amazing".

As she sipped a glass of water to bring her back to consciousness, the lady started to share her experiences of the session. She said she felt mum had experienced heart ache and that she had shifted some energy blocks around that area. She also said that she kept feeling her heart almost skipping a beat. Mum's jaw dropped open as she listened to the lady, she looked baffled. Funny how the universe eloquently speaks through others to get our attention isn't it?

After we had paid for the session, we left Cosmic Whispers and went to meet Lola and Bella in a coffee shop.

"Well, how did it go?" asked Lola.

Mum kept looking over her shoulder to check no one was listening. "It was really weird. The experience in itself was amazing, so relaxing but the lady mentioned my heart skipping a beat and that I had experienced heartache. Do you think she's been following us or has seen my Facebook post?" Always sceptical!

"How could that be possible? Do you think she was referring to Jim? Incidentally, how are you feeling about that now?" asked Lola.

"I'm okay. Oddly enough, it does feel like I've had some sort of peace come over me today, like some sort of closure on that relationship. They say time is a healer, maybe Reiki is too!"

"It's all a bit weird yet exciting isn't it. Maybe there's more to life than we think," said Lola.

You've a lot to learn, humans. I thought. But you are, and you will continue to learn if you should choose to.

"What time are you out dancing with Eve tonight?" Lola said, changing the subject. "Should we be heading back?"

Mum was going out dancing with her dance friend this evening, back to her Rock 'n' Roll. She hadn't been for a while, too worried about her heart with all the tests.

"Do you know? You've just triggered my mind. That's weird." said mum.

"Come on, let's walk and talk and you can tell me what's weird." said Lola as she stood up and picked up her coat off the back of the chair.

"I recall a very peculiar feeling from my Reiki session. I'm not sure if I was fully conscious but I know I wasn't asleep either, but at some point, I had a vision that I had received a message from Eve saying, 'I'm sat outside Lola's house.' How strange? She's not due until six and it's only three, ha, I'm such a worrier. Even when I'm meant to be relaxing, I worry about the future".

You sure do mum. You sure do.

As we pulled up outside Lola's house, there was Eve's car.

"That looks like Eve's car," said Lola.

"Can't be. She's not due for a couple more hours at least."

Just as mum said this, Eve jumped out of her car, smiling from ear to ear. "Sorry I'm early, I was in Milton Keynes' shopping centre and I got bored. I hope you don't mind me hanging out with you for a bit longer, I did send you a message."

Mum looked like she'd seen a ghost, and as she pulled out her phone, she saw the message from Eve, 'I'm sat outside Lola's house'.

There was a parallel universe in action. Mum was finally getting into flow, although I think it scared her a bit, her face said it all. The universe was once again speaking eloquently.

Masked personas

A few weeks later, life was settling back down. Back to the old mundane routine. Mum was putting her recent events down to 'nice experiences' and was slipping back into the unconscious world, the treadmill of 'doing' not 'being'.

The days she needed to go into the office, she would put her suit on for work and leave in the morning, coming home looking drained with no life in her eyes. I could see the sadness. She was definitely 'existing' and not really 'living'.

In the evenings mum would sit next to the log burner with Lola. They were always cold and had that thing ablaze, even in summer. It's a good job that I'm a fire spaniel at heart. The flames were therapeutic, almost like a form of energy dispersion and clearance. They would sit and watch the flames for hours, mesmerised, lost in thought. At least it was better for their soul than any of the news on the television. Both of them would exchange thoughts about their days. I sat, listened and observed. It was funny how most of the focus was on what had gone wrong, rather than what had gone right. Mum would tell Lola about conversations she'd had with colleagues, not daring to share her experiences from the weekend, the Reiki experience, or the dancing. When Lola challenged her and asked why, she simply said she was worried what people would think. Does this resonate with you? Too much time spent worrying about what others think to really embrace the happiness of the conversation? It's such a shame.

I was witnessing this more and more. Mum would always skirt around the edges. You could tell that she wanted to share these experiences, but that she was too fearful about what people might think or how they might judge her. She reserved them for Lola only. What was she afraid of when it came to letting her heart sing and leading with this in conversations?

It was crazy. Here was the universe delivering a clear strong message to mum, just to be 'herself' and she was delivering a clear strong message to everyone else as to how she was 'trying to fit in', scared of upsetting the apple cart.

This masked persona continued, but a double life seemed to be evolving. She could be the real her at weekends being drawn to the things that made her happy, the Reiki experience, for example, and yet she felt like she had to put an act on at work. What if she just embraced life and lived her working week like she did at weekends? Are they mutually exclusive? From where I sit it seems so amazingly simple. Of course, you can have the same level of happiness in your week as you do at the weekends, why couldn't you?

Tapping into eloquence

It was a Monday morning and mum came running down the stairs, late for work as always. However, there was a difference on this day, there was an excitement in her voice. This was unusual for a Monday morning. Mum would normally have 'Monday morning blues' and not display that 'Friday feeling'.

"Lola, I've just had an email from the lady at Cosmic Whispers. They're running a workshop this weekend and she's had two people cancel. She wondered if we wanted to attend the workshop in their place, and she's offered a 50% discount. What do you think?"

"Before I say yes, what am I letting myself in for?" said Lola.

"Something about talking to angels and the universe. After my last experience at Cosmic Whispers, it should be quite fun!" mum responded.

At least mum was now starting to listen to the nudges from the universe. Maybe it was the 50% discount that swayed the accountant in her?

The workshop weekend soon arrived and we were back at Cosmic Whispers. This time we were also accompanied by Lola and Bella.

We were invited into a big spacious room; it was an informal setting. Colourful yet calming, and with cushions scattered across the floor. There was peppermint and wild orange in the diffuser to lift everyone's energy, and there was chatter amongst the other participants, who were all so gentle and shy like mum.

Once we had registered, we were invited to sit on the floor and split up to meet someone new. I could see this both excited mum and put the fear into her. She loved talking to others and learning about them, yet she was shy and worried what they would think about her. There and then, that masked persona came into full force, catching her out again.

We sat with a lady who was bubbly and smiling, and had a gentle warmth to her. The leader invited our attention as she explained the activity we were going to embark on. The humans were to sit with some tarot or angel cards that were spread around the room, selecting the ones they were most drawn to. They would then pull out the card from shuffling the pack and just connect with their hearts and say what they saw.

Most of the room looked excitedly nervous and you could see that these people were worried about getting it wrong. When connected with universal energy, you cannot get it wrong in fact, it's the path of least resistance.

Mum's partner went first and as the lady pulled a card and started to talk, mum was stunned by the words that came flowing out of her mouth. Heart ache, wires, tests, brake-line pipe. This lady finished and said, "I'm sorry, I'm rubbish at this, it's all garble, perhaps I should take up knitting instead".

It never ceases to amaze me how eloquently the angels speak through a person, especially when that person is open to sharing a message. As garbled as the messages seem to the individual, often it's not to the person receiving. Mum reassured the lady that the message was not garbled and shared the story of the brake-line pipe going on the motorway and all her hospital tests. The lady quietly smiled as a mixture of relief passed across her face. I could see that the lady also questioned whether this message had just been a fluke. See! We all have our doubts, even when the evidence is presented to us.

Mum was next to go. As she pulled the card out, it turned out to be the number 11. Quite significant for the angels, but mum had yet to notice. She carried on reading the card to the lady, saying what she saw. Mum kept apologising saying that nothing was coming to her, red in the face and flustered. The leader noticed and came across to them both. "Oh, number 11. The angels are definitely with you, Ellen. Just drop to your heart and let the words flow." she advised.

It felt like a lifetime, but mum was soon on a roll, words tumbling out of her mouth, her eyes lit up with passion and excitement, her energy had shifted. She went on to tell the lady that her son was emigrating, possibly to Australia but she felt that that was too cliché, and that it was more likely to be Germany. Mum said that she felt he would receive a job offer and that the lady would be spending more time with him abroad.

As mum came to an abrupt halt, she let out a sigh and turned to the lady for feedback, almost cringing, her body language and her face screwed into a frown.

"You're a natural, my son went for a job in Australia but he has just recently accepted one in Germany."

"You're just saying that to make me feel good," said mum.

"Not at all. Look, I'll show you his text message," said the lady.

Mum looked gobsmacked as the lady withdrew her phone and presented the message. You humans have more intuition than you think you do. If only you took the path of least resistance and embraced the journey, you'd have less to figure out and more time to be stress-free.

The day went on and the leader was amazing. She demonstrated how to make a vision board. Her cork board was full of wonderful vibrant yet calming pictures of health, happiness, fun, and objects. A wonderful balance of everything the lady wanted to attract into her life, from cars to relationships, holidays, or that ideal career. She spoke knowingly of how having a vision board creates those thoughts and feelings in the now and how this helps to shape our reality and our future life.

During this, I heard Lola whisper to mum. "Surely that can't work?" Mum for once didn't respond, I think the jury was out. Hmm, I wondered, had the eloquent whispers stirred something in mum? Was she experiencing a shift?

As we left Cosmic Whispers and said our goodbyes, a shopping bag in hand, yes, mum had purchased some angel cards to practice with Lola at home, she was excitedly babbling on, her energy supercharged. "Wow! That was fun, but number 11, what on earth was the leader talking about? What have numbers got to do with anything?"

Oh, dear human, you do have a lot of growing to do. Numbers are significant for many reasons and if you keep spotting them, then the angels are trying to communicate with you Whether it's 11:11 on the clock, or a number 11 bus driving by. Number 11 represents an instinctive person, being the most intuitive number, signifying connection with a higher energy. Any number, a single digit, a repetition of numbers, 2 or 22, or 333. Simply google, spiritual meaning and 22 (insert the relevant number,) and interpret the message for yourself. I've a lot to teach humans. Sometimes I wonder if I'm Lord Louie or Lord Google.

Spiritual divide

Monday morning was back and as if by hypnosis, mum put on her dull grey suit and looked so sad. It's not an either-or situation, you don't have to hide away from the world, your gifts, your desires and what excites you to try and fit in, but this was what mum thought. It felt like she was living a double life, almost a spiritual divide between her heart and her head. How she thought others wanted her to show up, versus how the real her should be showing up. It's obvious to see in others, but not quite so in yourself. Let me ask you, do you feel aligned with your heart? Or does your head sometimes do the leading?

That evening mum returned home, almost lifeless, as if the energy had been sucked right out of her. She was born to do more than just pay the bills and be perceived as being 'successful' just because she had a good job. Her heart and her energy had sung at the weekend and now it was firmly buried, just like the cards she'd purchased at the weekend and slid into a drawer. It was as if she was packing away her heart with her cards and it broke my heart. If only I could speak and she could understand me.

Human eloquence

The see-saw of life was definitely inviting mum to play, although she wasn't quite leading with her heart yet. As she sat chatting with Lola, enjoying a midweek tipple and reminiscing about the weekend just gone, Lola invited mum to do a card reading and a smile appeared over mum's face. Thank goodness someone else was on my side, encouraging mum to connect with her heart. Lola was the best.

Mum went to the drawer and pulled out her cards. "I don't think I'll be able to do this, I know you too well, Lola."

"Of course, you can Ellen, just practice. It's only me and it's a bit of fun." Eloquently put Lola. Well done, I thought.

Mum invited Lola to pick three cards and as she did, mum stared at them. I could see she was connecting with her heart and she was off. She explained to Lola that she was going to meet an American man under a chance circumstance and it would be something to do with speaking or a message being shared. You could see Lola's eyes darting back and forth, intrigued. "It looks like you're going to be visiting America too," mum relayed, "And possibly a whirlwind romance."

Lola was howling with laughter, "Are you crazy, a whirlwind romance? I could maybe stretch a trip to America, but I'm just not the kind of woman to engage in a whirlwind romance."

Be careful, Lola. Life is sometimes full of surprises, I thought to myself.

Mum looked a little deflated at Lola's response, she was only saying what she saw. Just at that moment, the phone rang. It was my human grandparents, calling from Tyddyn Bach. Lola was still laughing and mum had started laughing at this point too, after all, this was meant to be a bit of fun. They proceeded to tell my grandparents, what had happened and before long everyone was laughing. Laughing is good for the soul. As mum came off the phone, she'd been reminded of our upcoming trip to Wales that weekend (she'd accidentally forgotten, and thankfully she had not double booked). A family gathering. I best get my dicky bow out, I thought smiling!

LORD LOUIE'S LESSONS

Eloquent messages are all around you.

1. Have you ever heard a song repeated on the radio and thought to yourself, that's annoying, it keeps playing? Next time, please take note and listen to the words. They may be whispering you a message.

2. Do you make time for yourself? Is it enough? Or do you also feel guilty about spending money on yourself? Are your decisions made on the basis that you are saving it for your family? Think about this instead, what are you teaching them from your approach, what behaviour are you demonstrating? If you can't pamper yourself, then how will they learn that it's okay for them to indulge? After all, they're watching and learning from you.

3. Take some time to reflect on times in your life when you have been trying to force the path that you 'think' you should be on. Have there been blockers in your way that have perhaps frustrated you? What else were you being invited to do at that moment? Were there whispers coming from somewhere else that you chose to put your fingers in your ears because you weren't ready?

4. Do you live a double life? Does your heart and soul speak to you eloquently yet you decide not to listen to it?

5. What eloquent messages are you receiving right now, this week, this day, this hour? If you stop and listen, you'll start to see, hear and notice them. I invite you to trust your heart and whatever you believe in, the angels, the universe, God, a higher energy, it's there for you to align and connect with and I promise it will guide you.

6. Just sit down with a pen and paper and ask the angels what you need to know. Write. Write anything and keep practicing until it flows so fast from your pen that you can't keep up and you've no idea where these thoughts are pouring out from. Go on... I dare you!

Eloquence

Through eloquence we speak
To those we meet
On our travels
To everyone we greet

We whisper to you
Every single day
We've heard your dreams
Come on, let's play

For life is too short
You watch it float by
We're here to help
Please listen, hear our cry

Life is magical
It's a pure gift
Put back up your sails
Don't let your boat drift

Signs all around
We invite you to look
Is it a course, a conversation?
Or even a book?

Take time, slow down
Notice what you see
Take time to understand
The signs, gifted from me

Repetitive numbers
Books or a bird
Landing in front of you
A clue to be heard

A book may fall
From a shelf above
Or out on a dog walk
A sight of a dove

Turn to a page
And read on cue
Look up the dove meaning
And see the next clue

Tune into our whispers
We speak eloquently
Just open your eyes
Take a look and you'll see

chapter 3

SIGNIFICANCE

"Being significant; importance; noteworthiness".

Oxford English Dictionary

Buried treasure

W/e had arrived in Wales. I woke up after a restful sleep. Nana and Gramps's pillows are much more comfortable than mum's but shhh! I wouldn't tell her that, it may hurt her feelings. She's a sensitive soul and takes a lot to heart.

In Wales, there's so much to see and do. First, I always run through to see Nana and Gramps to greet them and show them how much I love them. Then I bunny hop down the stairs, past the guardian angel sign that speaks to everyone who passes it. It's a little mirror which sits on a corner table at the half landing. Beautiful words written on the front stating and reading, 'She watches over you each day, with warm and loving care. This little angel guides your steps, she's with you everywhere.' I thank the angels for my wonderful life, before running free in the garden. This is subject to a human opening the door, but mostly someone will oblige. Reader – do you release excitement regularly? I do hope you don't just reserve it for special occasions! Don't worry if you do, we'll explore that more later.

That morning the sun was just rising over the mountain top, casting long shadows across the lush green garden, the blades of grass glistening with the morning dew. It was a beautiful blue sky with the light peeking through the curtains, tantalising the senses to gently stir us. My human was still fast asleep. I whimpered quietly to gently wake her. Whenever we come to Wales, I just can't contain my excitement, it just bubbles up inside me. If I'm honest, I feel this way most days and I know this feeling shouldn't be reserved just for holidays. Do you?

The air that morning was fresh and warm with a soft breeze brushing past my fur. The sweet smell of flowers gently moving in the morning air was everywhere and perhaps a whiff of fox poo that I could find to roll in later. My thoughts were with my mum and I decided it was going to be THE best day of our lives.

Come on, wake up. We've got an exciting day ahead of us... oooh she moved. Maybe she's awake. Please, please, please!

"Louie, shhh, Nana and Gramps are asleep, it's only 7 am. Why can't you just lay in, we had a long drive yesterday and a busy week at work. I'm tired and I just want to sleep a little longer, please, just one more hour Louie."

Well, I wasn't going to accept that. I really didn't care; I've had all the feelings bubbling inside me. We'd woken up with the gift of life and mum was just being grumpy and tired. I don't know. You humans bury all your treasured feelings in your chest and seldom release them. Why don't you ever just jump out of bed and celebrate the coming day? The last time I saw this happen was on Christmas Day with the children in the extended family. Do you remember those times? When you were a child and Christmas Day was so magical, feelings just tumbled out with the expectancy of the day, from the moment you opened your eyes. The presents hadn't been opened, but the feelings had been released, the actual present wasn't the physical gift but the gift you gave yourself in choosing to release those feelings. What happens to them the other 364 days of the year when you become an adult? Even on Christmas Day some of you won't release the joy. Have you forgotten how to release these wonderful feelings? You **are** significant and your feelings **are** important. Humph. I'll just have another nap...

Pink wellington boots

Later that day we took a walk with Nana up the mountain, past an old Roman Road. Isn't history just fascinating? Our ancestors actually walked this piece of land. The views were incredible and when I stood on top of the rocks, I caught the breeze in my fur, just like the scene out of Titanic, but with a happier ending.

Mum often pulls out her phone to take pictures for memories. Some make them onto Facebook, others don't. It depends whether in the moment, she's worrying about others judging her or not.

"Just sit there on the rocks Ellen, with Louie, and I'll take your picture," said Nana.

I could see mum looking coy and I knew exactly what she would be thinking. Admittedly it was a bit of a fashion disaster, as I looked at her standing there in her red Wales rugby shirt and illuminous pink wellies, hair scraped back, but hey, who cares what we look like, it's what's inside that counts. You could see her mind flick from the thought of just being herself, free and happy with only sheep and horses to pass view on her, to the thought of uploading a photo on Facebook for the whole world to pass judgement, good or bad, and it was a 'no go'. Do you worry what others will think? What is your fear?

"Maybe tomorrow." Mum said to Nana.

Mum does worry too much about what others think. I knew I had a bit of coaching work to do in this area with her. Did I forget to mention that whilst mum thinks I am dependent on her, she is actually dependent on me? I am her personal hot water bottle, chaperone, guard dog and not to mention my role as her coach. Even when she's not looking all glammed up, I can tell you that she is naturally beautiful to me. If only she could have seen it. That also goes for all of you readers out there. I promise you that you are all naturally beautiful inside and out. Now there's a compliment - please RECEIVE it.

For goodness' sake mum, just have your picture taken. Nana will not take no for an answer so you might as well just embrace it and create the memory as a reminder of good times. Why do humans always worry so much about what you look like and what other people think? Seriously, I just smile and look fabulous, even when I am knee deep in mud. I don't care that my blonde legs are now black in silt. It's about being in the moment!!

I could see what was happening before mum could see it herself. She's a unique human being. There's no one like her on the planet with her unique special skills, yet she was settling for a life that she put a ceiling on. Too often she stayed in her comfort zone to avoid upsetting people, including herself, to avoid being judged, in her eyes, for being a failure of living this 'perfect' life, to avoid disappointing herself and her family. Now there's a lot of pressure trying to spin a lot of plates. There is only one plate to spin and that was her own happiness. Once she found this plate, all of the others would naturally spin around her.

Nana eventually coerced mum into having our photo taken. She's not yet put that one on Facebook! Plenty of me, but with her behind the camera! Sound familiar? I'll keep you updated as to whether or not the photo makes it. I'm working on it, if only I could master the laptop!

Party time

Later that afternoon, it was party time. No specific reason to celebrate. Just because the extended family hadn't gotten together for a while. I don't think they really knew what they were actually celebrating was life. Such a precious gift that isn't celebrated enough. Humans seem to be happier when there is an opportunity to come together and celebrate. This is amazing, but I do wish you would be happier just because. Party or no party. I loved this type of celebration, observing everyone laughing and joking, really being in the moment.

It was an extra special day for me because my best friend, Buddy, was attending the party. He's my special cousin. Although similar in genes, he's a little different and another earth angel in disguise as a Cavajack. A special mix of a Cavalier King Charles Spaniel and a Jack Russell. We make a really good team when we're together, it's an opportunity to bounce ideas off each other, as to how we can best serve the humans.

My best human friend David, was in charge of the BBQ. His name was very apt given we were in Wales – as to me he was a Saint. Ha! Get it? Saint David, although he's not Welsh, he's a saint at cooking the BBQ. For fun he was wearing a personalised apron that had a picture of me sitting next to a BBQ waiting for the sausages to cook. Sometimes you've just got to put the fun into the moment because if you don't, who else will?! I could see all the guests smiling when they noticed the apron. Love is all around us if we choose to feel and accept it. You see, there are two ways you can look at having your picture up at a party, either cringe with embarrassment or feel the love. I'm choosing to feel the love, looking at the picture of me on the apron. Which feels better to you?

We were coming into autumn and fortunately the weather gods were still on our side. The food was laid on the table out in the garden, and the humans mingled and chatted enjoying the sunny afternoon.

"Nooooooo!" Shouted Nana as she saw a squirrel shoot down the tree and across the middle of the table. Chaos ensued, humans were screaming and running away but Buddy came to the rescue. His terrier instinct saved the day and shooed the squirrel away. I love that he has this skill, it wasn't one I acquired but that's okay, that's what makes us unique.

No comparing, just embracing and harnessing skills of loved ones around us. David on the BBQ, Buddy on squirrel watch and me having my moment of fame on an apron. You humans are unique too and possess skills to complement one another. I hope you're harnessing the teams around you and complementing your amazing with their amazing. What are your unique skills? And, don't even start to tell me you have none!

The evening was perfect and after the mini episode of chaos, everything settled, just like life. It's the law.

Create your dreams

The next morning mum was in full flow. She was reeling off the excitement of talking to relatives yesterday and a conversation that had challenged her norm around her job.

"Louie, sitting here now, thinking about what I want to achieve for us, I just know life will be amazing when I'm doing my dream job, if not a coach, then what? When I've paid the mortgage and I'm financially free, I'll be able to relax then, I will be 'there'."

She had a big smile on her face as she got lost in thought. She often talks to me. Do you, or people you know do this with your earth angels, your pets?

Now here's the thing about what mum just said. Nothing physically changed in that moment, only a thought, yet you could tell she was enjoying the feeling already. Magical hey? Wouldn't it be great if you humans learnt to control your thoughts more, so you could experience and embrace those magical moments, having the thoughts and feelings before life has actually caught up with you? Well, maybe you can! Maybe your dreams are more worthy and significant than you give them credit for.

At that point mum really was disillusioned, believing that amazing was a destination you reach when you achieve something. Where is 'there' anyway? You humans think you'll be there or to term it differently, 'happy when…'. Happy when you've paid off your mortgage; happy when you've found out that you've gotten the job or passed the exam; happy when you've met your dream partner; happy when it's Friday so you can enjoy the weekend. Why wait? I don't! Maybe you can learn HOW to stop waiting too. But, more on this later.

There is hope. I just want you to know that it's possible. You don't have to believe me, but please trust me. I am loving the life I want to live. I am happy and relaxed, I am 'there'. Wherever there is, that you humans say you'll get to. I wished at that point mum could be 'there' too. She lives too much in the future, in fear of not having enough, coming from a place of lack rather than abundance, or in the past, with regret for what she could've done or should've, or would've done differently. She was blind-sided. I just know I have everything I need and more and when I do, it's as if by magic more abundance appears. Watch this. I bet if I use the power of my mind now and visualise cooked sausages, I'll receive them very, very soon. I've just placed my order with cosmic Amazon and as I sit back in the moment and trust, I know they will arrive.

Later that afternoon Nana woke up in her chair. Now here's my time to move, harnessing the law of attraction. If you're not familiar with this, then listen up. Everything in the universe is energy, even our thoughts. The principles of the law of attraction are, what you focus on (think), you attract. Whatever is showing up in your life right now is a mirror of your past thoughts. Earth shattering, hey? Don't be too despondent if you're not manifesting what you want in your life. A simple place to start is with a shift in thought. Focus on what you want, rather than what you don't want! Just like mum, she dislikes being an accountant, but every day she woke up and thought to herself, I'm an accountant, what do I have to do today, so she repeated the thoughts and seldom (until now) thought about her future. So, by virtue of the law of attraction, guess what she keeps getting? An accounting job!

You're an advanced species, you don't order from an online shop and question whether or not it will arrive. You just believe that it's on its way. So, why can't you do the same with life? Often, I see you humans focus on why you can't have something rather than what you want to have. A new car, you say? Okay, says the law of attraction in response to your order. Sadly, what you humans then do is cancel your order with the universe by focusing on the lack of money to pay for it, doubting you can have it. Why do you need to work out how that car will get to you? That's the universe's job, not yours. All you need to do is simply place the order and BELIEVE. The magic of the universe will decide the quickest way to get it to you, through winning a competition, a lease deal advert you've never seen before that makes it affordable, or perhaps a promotion at work that now comes with a company car. The options are endless, yet you cancel the order when you stop BELIEVING and start thinking of all the reasons why you can't have it. Make sense? Does this sound familiar? It's not just about the car, it's about life and your dreams. You can create the life you want, based on the thoughts you have. Please re-read that last sentence and say it out loud. Start focusing on what you want, rather than what you don't want! It's a powerful shift.

"Louie, I don't want to be an accountant forever, my car is old, I don't want to battle with starting it every day and not knowing if it's going to get me to work or not."

Perfect timing mum, see what she did there? She had a lot to learn too. She was telling me what she didn't want, rather than what she did. Perhaps if she had said, 'I would like to be of service to people, inspiring them to change and have a reliable wonderful car to drive so I can service my clients', then the universe might have a fighting chance of executing her order!

I too wanted a new car, I'd rather not pray to the angels on the motorway again, if I can avoid it.

Back to sausages! You see, the law of attraction works its magic, but only if you first 'show up'. You can't just sit and meditate and expect the sausages or the car to always come to you. I walk back and forth to the door, showing the universe that I'm willing to move in the direction of my dreams. Yes! Nana was moving, I skipped to the fridge and sat expectantly waiting for it to open! My Nana is the best, she's like the best cosmic Amazon delivery person in the world, and somehow, she always knows what I want. If it's a car you want, look for your perfect car, visualise it, test drive it, show the universe you're ready to receive it.

"Louie, no more sausages… okay, last one." says Nana.

Yippee – the power of manifestation at work and that, my reader friend is how you make dreams happen! If only I could teach mum.

Stirrings of awakening

As the day went on mum started to share her thoughts again. "Louie, remember the Cosmic Whispers workshop and when the lady talked about the vision board – what if life is a game? Shall we have some fun and see if we can attract something?"

I knew something was brewing! Maybe her consciousness is stirring.

"Louie, let's go shopping, I need a vision board!" exclaimed mum.

I feel this is the start of something, I have absolutely no idea where this is going now. Maybe I'll just close my eyes and play deaf, if I pretend, I'm asleep then maybe she'll go without me.

"Come on Louie, let's pop you in the car in your harness."

As she puts my harness on, I know I'm in for an afternoon of chaperoning at the shops!

After several hours of traipsing around the shops, we had a pair of shoes, another pair of shoes! Apparently, they were too much of a bargain to leave in the shop, even though I am not sure when she will get to wear them. Most days she's rocking her slippers, wellies or trainers to walk my good self... stilettos don't quite work walking over fields.

We also had some crystals from the crystal shop. Apparently, she liked the ones in Cosmic Whispers and wished she'd bought them. The lady invited her to use her intuition and just pick ones she was drawn to. Great advice! It's definitely the best way to select crystals - or do they select you? Just like choosing a companion! She doesn't know it yet, but she picked rose quartz, which is for love, including self-love, such a beautiful crystal to start with and amazing to help her heal her heart. She also picked amethyst which is very grounding and great for rest, calmness and stillness. Maybe that will calm her agitated mind!

And... finally, we made it to the shop we were meant to be going to all along, and purchased a vision board. I couldn't wait to see what she was going to do with that. Honestly, she's not been the most creative of beings to date, but humans can and do change.

Designing your future life

Having got back to the farm, I took the opportunity to curl up and go to sleep. Suddenly there were three loud bangs on the front door which made me jump out of my skin from my slumber and I was soon at the front door barking before I even realised what had happened. It's amazing how quickly adrenaline can work. OMG! We're under attack, the postman has arrived. I swear all postmen are out to get us. Mum says they are delivering us gifts, but they always make a loud bang at the door when I'm asleep. If I was a cat, I'd have relinquished all of my nine lives by now.

"Ooh Louie perfect timing, some printer ink so I can get to work on my vision board. Now let's see, what would I like to attract into my life? Well firstly, a decent man. Maybe that's too much of a stretch, surely at my age all the decent ones have been taken? Especially after my experience with Jim. What a waste of time that relationship was."

Now, now! I thought, the first rule of thumb is to expect miracles and not be negative. Tut tut! Have I not taught you anything? Just as I mentioned earlier, thoughts become things! A vision board simply won't work if you're thinking it's unlikely to come true. Talking about Jim, some people just come into your life for a reason or a season, not everyone is meant to stay. It wasn't a waste, mum enjoyed some happy times with him and he did introduce her to Lola, so there were some positives.

"I guess I can't tarnish all men with the same brush, I'm learning to trust. So, let's see. Hmmm, maybe someone who is tall, dark and handsome, must be rich…"

That's a bit fickle. Don't forget, it's not just about what you include but what you forget to include. Be very careful. You may get someone tall, dark and handsome and rich, but if you forget loyal and trustworthy then you may just get another Jim! Keep it broad. What is your ultimate goal and how will that feel? I sit staring at mum, she looks perplexed, almost as if she is hearing my question - if you could wave a magic wand mum, what would it be?

I desire a loving harmonious relationship that is perfect for me. Not only do I want to have a good relationship with my partner but I'd also like to have a good relationship with myself, truly value myself. Is that possible?"

Yes! This is it. I could jump for joy with pride. The printer reels off two pictures. One of a couple looking happy and connected and one with a picture of a girl smiling, looking happy, emanating joy.

"Ooh, I know. I'd love to go to California in May next year. Mike Dooley, who writes notes from the universe and teaches the law of attraction is scheduled to do an event, how cool would that be? America! Though Louie, it's so inconceivable, I'm kidding myself, aren't I? Not only will I be unlikely to get time off work, I can't justify paying all that money."

Here we go again, time for me to coach her through my knowing look. She was trying to attract things into her life yet, her negative thoughts were stopping her from believing it was truly possible. I stared intently with my head tilted and listened as she continued on with the reasons why she couldn't. However, all of a sudden there was a breakthrough… or at least a mini one.

"Blow it. I'll print it anyway, maybe dreams can come true! I'll just try it, I'll focus on what I want," mum said.

Yes! She'd finally got it. I was so pleased.

Maybe I should think about a career change and start living my dream career. How about my independent accounting firm's senior partner who wants to retire and as a result of this, given he has no one to leave the business to, we get taken over by a huge multinational, we move abroad, or I get made redundant and live happily ever after. That would work".

Are you sure about this mum? Are you really ready for relocation or redundancy? Your accountancy firm is tiny, no one has even heard of them. Before she had listened to my communicative looks, she'd printed 'relocation or redundancy' and stuck it on her vision board. Be careful what you wish for mum, I thought. I hoped with all my heart that the relocation ones would come off and that it would lead to somewhere nice for me to run in the fields!

Hey, wait! What am I going to do whilst you go on a jolly to America? I do hope you can get me a passport. If only I could print something for the vision board too!

I watched her chuckling to herself and printing off lots of paper and cutting out pictures before she pinned them to the board. I was fascinated in what mum was actually thinking while doing this as she had gone quiet. I wonder what the microphone is for, I thought, and by the law of attraction I must've paid a virtual penny for her thoughts because she did just that and shared them with me.

"Louie, wouldn't it be great if we could share our experiences one day, from the depths of despair hurtling down the motorway to the subsequent events at Cosmic Whispers. Everything happens for a reason and perhaps sharing our experiences would give hope to the world that there is something more, whether it's Reiki or something else."

That's a nice thought mum. I think you'd be a good human earth angel. We could be a duo of earth angels, bringing joy and hope to the world.

Sometime later I realised that I must have nodded off and the thing that woke me was the sound of the fridge door opening. Oooh, someone is in the kitchen. I must investigate.

"Louie – seriously, I've just printed that and you've stepped all over it."

Chill! I'm just helping, it looks better with paw indents on it. Lighten up, have some fun, it's only a little mud. You humans really sweat the small stuff too often.

As mum sat back and looked at the board, she declared it was finally finished. A work of art with her future dreams, desires and wishes. She looked excited and alive again, and there was almost hope and joy in her eyes. The glimmers of happiness, ever since that fateful day at Cosmic Whispers, were starting to bud.

"Why have I never done this before Louie? We set ourselves goals at work and loosely at home, maybe we hope to get married or own a car or a house but do we live deliberately and focused? I'd say I've been living accidentally up until now."

Oh, charming. So, you think I'm an accident? Well, maybe I ordered you on my 'virtual' vision board. The angels sent me to help guide you in life. They sent me on a mission telling me that I had to be your angel in disguise, so I don't believe in accidents, more gifts in disguise. Who and what are gifts in disguise in your life?

Please can we go for a walk now?

"Louie please stop pawing me, what do you want?"

Seriously, you've been sitting for ages, can't we just play now?

"Okay, okay, Louie. Just two minutes, I forgot to add my red convertible car…"

Over-egged significance

I just love the anticipation of leaving the house, going out into the big wide world, not knowing who I'll meet on that journey. I became increasingly excited as mum got my lead and harness in readiness for our adventures and, on that day, I was super excited that we may be off to the forest. I just love the trees and all the wonderful smells, the sound of the leaves blowing in the wind, being surrounded by nature just listening to the birds tweet. I know my mum loves it there too. I notice how she slows down and smiles. I can see her body relax as she melts into nature, away from the craziness of the busy world. As Nana climbed into the car, I remember thinking how great it would be for all of us to go to the woods that day.

After a long walk in the woods, we got back to the warmth of the car. I was excited to go home and sit on Gramps' knee by the log burner, but that thought was interrupted as mum announced that our next stop was not home, but the shops.

"We're just going by the shops Louie to get some food; you stay strapped in and be a good boy. It won't be much longer before we're home."

Why do humans always say 'I won't be long'? Whether they're gone for ten minutes or four hours? Seems a bit odd to me. I don't understand why she doesn't just tell me she'll be home at whatever time. At least I would be able to plan my naps and play hide the slipper accordingly.

As we pulled into the supermarket, my Nana jumped out of the car, all in a fluster because there was a queue. I could see her body language change and her stress levels rise. If only she knew how to control her emotions. Mum and I waited patiently in the car. I just love being with my mum, it doesn't matter where or what we're doing, I'm just happy.

It's sad to see the ebbs and flows of life, stealing away the joy from people and almost turning them into programmed robots. Society says 'in this situation' you *must* think, feel and act in this way. It's ludicrous. Whatever happened to choosing? I wish my humans would take a moment and just be. It's just a queue, there is no need to get stressed or rush. Just enjoy chatting to people in the queue, enjoy the moment. What could be that difficult?

As Nana came out of the supermarket, she was carrying a bag full of groceries and then placed them on the back seat with me.

On our drive home we rounded a corner and I could see a disaster about to strike. There were eggs, balancing precariously on top of the bag. I sat quietly, listening to Nana and mum talking, moaning about the traffic and the person that just cut them up. Seriously guys I thought to myself, can't you just let it go. You're using up good energy on a situation that happened ages ago and quite frankly, you're interrupting my peace with your negative energy. Oh no, oh no, oh no, the eggs! Crash on the floor they went. Ah well. This would be interesting to see how they would react when we arrived home.

We pulled up to the driveway, the gravel grinding underneath the wheels of the car. Usually, I could always tell when we were near home from the sounds and the smells. Although, at that point, all I could smell was egg.

As mum opened the back door to release me, her face dropped. "Aw no, no, no, no, no." she cried, as if it was the end of the world. "Quick!" she shouted to Nana, "The eggs have gone everywhere, it's a disaster - the car is going to stink."

Nana started beating herself up "Oh no, I'm so sorry, it was my fault. I shouldn't have left the eggs on top of the bag, I'm so stupid! What an idiot."

Why do humans do this? It was a complete accident and yet they feel the need to berate themselves, again using up good energy. My Nana is so kind, she would never say this to anyone else, yet she says it to herself. It really breaks my heart. But the thing is, all you humans have done it. Spoken to yourselves like you would never speak to your best friend. You are your own worst enemies sometimes. What happened to being your own cheerleaders, exuding self-confidence and encouragement? Ah, I hear you, 'society says it's being big headed'. Well, what if society was wrong? Is it really working for you? Everyone builds you up, for you to firmly tear yourself back down. Sounds a bit defeatist to me.

Several hours later, mum and Nana flopped on the sofa exhausted. Having cleaned the car which now smelt fresh again and with a few of the eggs surviving their fall, there were no major dramas. When all is said and done, it really doesn't actually matter - we arrived home safely, the car was cleaned, and I got special time with Gramps by the log burner. Why do humans sweat the small stuff? Is it really that significant that the egg drama had to take over the amazing walk in the woods? Which would you choose to focus on, and which do you think you would feel better from focussing on? In my eyes it's simple, why can't it be in yours?

Results day

The dreaded results day. Mum HATED this. She worried so much about what people would think if she had failed her final accountancy exams. How bizarre! She seemed to have forgotten that she had already proved she could pass nine of them, so what was another three, for goodness' sake?! To be honest people don't really care anyway. Too wrapped up in worrying about what others think of them. Ha! Well, that's just silly in itself, isn't it?

Being in Wales for a long weekend at least meant that mum wasn't sitting in the office on a Monday morning, waiting for the email to ping through and this helped somewhat with her anxiety. I could tell it was playing on her mind. She'd hardly slept the night before, even though she had her rose quartz crystal tucked under her pillow. She'd read that this was good for love and calmness, and to just intuitively pick up the crystal you were drawn to in that moment and place it where you felt comfortable. The energy of the crystal would do the rest to support you.

"Any news love?" Nana asked.

"No, please can you stop asking!" Mum bit Nana's head off.

Come on mum, that's not kind, she's only being supportive. I could see mum was anxious and now that was spilling out into conversations and the energy in the house.

At that moment, there was a 'ping'. Mum froze. Why was she expecting the worst? She hasn't quite grasped the concept of daring to celebrate in advance, rather than worry!

"I've passed, I'm a qualified accountant." and there it was. Result first, feeling of excitement and relief second. This is completely the wrong way round, but mum has a lot to learn still. Does happiness really have to depend on outcomes? I don't want her or you to live your lives like this.

"Shall we bake a cake to celebrate? We always enjoyed doing that together when you were growing up!" said Nana.

Great idea – reigniting fun and creativity.

"Yes, why not?" said mum with a big grin on her face.

Significance of life

Later that evening, mum was staring at her vision board, and I could tell that she was replaying recent events since the Cosmic Whispers' experience.

"Louie, I've been thinking."

I best wriggle into a comfortable position and put my coaching ears on. Mum often has conversations with me. I hope you are able to do that as well? As I've said, us four legged friends, aka earth angels are always ready to listen.

Mum continued, "Quite often I think 'people like us' don't own private yachts or get to have time freedom. We were taught in school to work hard, get an education or an occupation, and get a well-paid job. To do 50 odd years in a job, and if you're one of the lucky ones, you'll love your job. Those jobs are few and far between and anyway society says you have to be really lucky to get one of these."

Yep, we're in for the long haul, I thought. I settled down poised and ready to listen as she continued.

"Since the incident on the motorway with the brakes failing, it's really made me think and I feel like I'm facing a life sentence of years just trundling along. I'm good at my accountancy practice job, (especially now that I'm qualified). The people are lovely, but we sit in an office, all five employees, and it's like Groundhog Day.

What am I doing with my life?! I'm half lucky that I can put up with my job to pay the bills and afford to go on holiday for five weeks of the year. But even that is signed off at the mercy of our director - he's lovely by the way, but being such a small firm, it's not always easy to get time off when other people are off and then we're at the mercy of the weather gods - praying the week we've managed to book for holiday will be sunny and warm. We're programmed to think that is acceptable!"

Wow, is she finally questioning the significance of her life after passing all those exams? Oh, my goodness, there's more...

"We dream of winning the lottery to escape, but what if there is another way? A way where we don't have to stack our odds waiting for a 1 in 45 million **chance** to win the lottery, or to be happy. This is crazy. What if we've been programmed to put a ceiling on our dreams based on what we think we can have or have achieved so far, instead of what we would love to have or want to achieve? And who am I to say it's not possible if I don't try?! How do we know we can't climb a mountain if we don't try? How do we know we can't learn a language if we don't take classes? Maybe society says 'it's too hard to learn a language as an adult' so, we automatically put the ceiling really low. In fact, it's not a ceiling, it's a floor that's cemented us firmly to the spot. How dare we move and try? Society said it would be hard."

Well! I wasn't expecting that surge of excitement, hope and optimism. She's got my attention now. Finally, she is starting to open her eyes, starting to believe what may be possible. I love these thoughts she's having. She doesn't realise it yet, but she's starting to shape her future – for the better.

LORD LOUIE'S LESSONS – THERE'S SOME BIG ONES HERE. GRAB A QUIET SPACE AND A PEN AND ALLOW YOURSELF SOME TIME TO REFLECT!

1. Your feelings matter and are of significance to you. What feelings are important to you and when was the last time you released them?
2. How often do you filter what you put on social media or indeed how you 'show up' when you leave your house? Do you have to put make-up on, dress up, present yourself, or are you just comfortable and happy in your own skin?
3. Do you worry about what people think? If so, why?
4. Are you spinning lots of plates, trying to keep everyone happy and everything going, yet forgetting THE most important plate, which is YOU? It may be a truth bomb, but one I want you to hear.
5. When was the last time you dared to dream about your future? Have you created a vision board? Do you truly feel deserving of your dreams? Don't worry if not, more of this to come later.
6. Are you your biggest champion or do you berate yourself?
7. Do you know what the significance of your life is? Have you ever stopped to think about that? Are you truly raising that ceiling? If you don't keep raising the bar on the

high jump, then do you really know what heights you can possibly reach?

8. What if you never get these opportunities again but instead of choosing fear, you choose love and that helps you grow and connect with your heart's true desires?

9. If you knew money wasn't an issue but you still had to work, what would you do?

10. Are you placing significance on thoughts and beliefs that serve you and help you to shine, or ones that keep you firmly cemented to playing small?

Significance

The significance of life
Is there to see
If only, you're open
To what's meant to be

For sometimes we think
It's not part of our plan
Yet we're on this road
Not sure, I'm a fan

With all the twist and turns
We must, let it be
For when the beauty unfolds
In all its glory, for us to see

Learn to embrace
What's here and now
Don't try to figure out
The blessed how

Your journey is unique
To who you are
Open your eyes
And you will go far

No longer resist
Or fight the path
Listen and learn
To what thou hath

Your life is important
So are your dreams
You matter the most
To others it seems

Listen up dear one
This message is for you
The rest of your life
Can change, now too

Your life is significant
Shine like a star
Light the way for others
Everyone near and far

chapter 4

DISCOVERY –
FINDING YOU

'the process of finding information, a place, or
an object, especially for the first time'

Cambridge Dictionary

Something missing

After a wonderful weekend in Wales, we were back at Lola's and back into the swing of work. We had made it to the weekend again.

As mum awoke, she started her usual chatter. Chatter always throws big questions or opinions about your life and your day ahead, even before you have gotten out of bed in the morning. Sound familiar?

"Thank goodness it's Saturday Louie. I am tired, and I feel like there is something missing in my life. Is it a boyfriend? Although, I do not want another Jim! Maybe if I change my career, I'll feel happier? Maybe when we move to Caernarvon Close, I'll be happier then, in our own home. Or maybe I just need a holiday...? If only I knew which bit to fix first. Life can be exhausting sometimes, it's like that pop-up fair game, Whac-A-Mole.

Here we go again. Time for me to put on my coaching hat and I've not even got out of bed yet.

As mum pulled back the curtains to reveal a cold crisp winter's day, I felt truly blessed and grateful, pretty much the complete opposite to how she was feeling. Funny that! I always sneak up in the middle of the night and curl up on the pillow next to her. I've learnt that to be a human you lay with your head on the pillow, so I do just the same. I think she finds it quite amusing and she often tells her friends that I forget I'm a dog. Well let me tell you, we're far more intuitive than you think we are, just because we can't talk doesn't mean we can't speak or even understand. I don't think mum realises that 55% of communication comes from body language so I know exactly when she's sad, happy, aggrieved and here's the thing, so does the subconscious mind of all humans - even though humans may not realise it.

You humans do it all the time when you walk into a room and you can just 'feel' the energy. You always know if someone has been arguing or is sad, even without a word being spoken out loud. Sometimes the energy is high and you just know that person is excited, which in my experience is a feeling, humans sadly reserve most for special occasions.

But, why? There is so much joy to be taken from each day, so much to be grateful for. Yet humans sometimes focus on the wrong things. There is the saying, 'what you focus on you find', no wonder your perception of your reality is skewed - you're looking through a blackened lens. You should try some rainbow lenses and see if you can see some things in colour! I dare you, go on. Humour me.

As mum walked towards the bathroom that morning, she momentarily stopped to look in the mirror. She scanned her body to see who was looking back at her. I jumped off the bed with a spring in my step to join her at the mirror and begin my first coaching session of the day. Looking into the mirror with mum I could see an earth angel (me!) and a beautiful human being standing together. While we were in black and white, looking back at us was a picture of health, beauty, opportunity and talent in both a unique human and a gorgeous dog. Oh my gosh! My eyelashes look amazing today and I'm looking quite trim, even if I do say so myself. I'm ready for the day.

"Aw Louie, my little shadow beside me. You sit looking up at me with your gorgeous brown eyes and fluffy ears, expectant of the day ahead. I wish I could be half as beautiful and happy in the morning. At least I know you love me Louie, and unconditionally so. Well, most of the time. Just not when I'm cooking you steak or cutting up cheese, then it may be a case of cupboard love. I just wish that I felt the same about myself. Why don't I like myself? Why is it that every time I look in the mirror, I scan my body and find all the imperfections as opposed to the bits that I love, or do I even have any?" As mum turned to look at me, I thought to myself, I know who is wearing the blackened lenses and who is wearing the rainbow lenses. Ironic, given that I can only see in black and white, don't you think?

I wish mum could see what I can see. A kind, caring, loving, beautiful human being - like no other. If only she could realise that love starts with self-love. You can only give what you've got and if you don't have any self-love, how can you give unconditional love to others? I find it fascinating that no one can be my mum better than she can; she's the only version of her in the world!! Even identical twins have different personalities and skills. I think that's pretty incredible. Out of 7.5 billion people in the world, NO ONE can be who she is better than she can, and she can't see it... yet. Do you have difficulty seeing this, and do you only see it in others but not yourself?

Over the years, I've heard mum say that she was taught that self-praise is no praise, and that if she thought she was a good person, then she was being big headed. Yet, this perspective doesn't work for her. She spends many a day being humble, batting off compliments whilst feeling embarrassed, yet she's amazing at giving compliments and praise. It's just crazy. Are you really telling me that you could give compliments to everyone else in the whole world, but not yourself? Have a think about this one for a minute. Does it make sense to you? Do you resonate with this? I hope not, otherwise I have more work to do.

"Louie, is this it? Is this my life? Working 9-5, eating, sleeping and getting five weeks of holiday a year? I feel pretty rubbish, like my light is dimming and I'm only young. At least I have you, Louie. Who needs a man?"

Exactly! I don't know where he would sleep for a start because after my long days coaching you, I sure as heck am not giving up my side of the bed! Boy, do I need my sleep to recharge, and you think you're exhausted? However, you are right. You don't need anyone or anything to complete you. I hope you realise that? You are special as you are.

Sometimes, I really wish I could speak so I could tell mum how life is really meant to be, to stop all her low-level pain and suffering, and get her to start living and being in the moment where the magic is.

"There's just something missing Louie, I know it! Is it the job? Maybe if I change jobs then I'll be happy! Maybe it's where we live, Louie. Do we want to live closer to the sea? Maybe that's it. Maybe it's not Caernarvon Close after all?" On and on she went, looping back around.

Well, I wouldn't say no to residing closer to the sea but, you're kidding yourself if you think that changing where we live will provide you with eternal happiness. Temporarily changing external things such as a house, location, a job, or a holiday may give you a temporary boost in your feelings, but it never lasts because wherever you go, there you are. You cannot get away from your negative chatter, mum. Even when you are on holiday and the sun is shining, fear and worry don't go away, and the chatter is just about different things - being eaten by a shark or getting lost in a foreign place. These are all things that go through mum's head. Is it the same for you, reader?

The last time mum went on holiday, the Friday before she went, she had the 'Friday feeling' even though she'd managed to negotiate working from home that day which I was very pleased about, it meant extra company and trips to the fridge which were a total win-win for me. The morning of the holiday, mum had the 'holiday happiness' feeling and then the day she returned, she had 'Monday morning blues' on the Sunday night!

Does this resonate with you? Are you always chasing feelings? Always trying to get that next pot of gold at the end of the rainbow. Human beings may be able to put a man on the moon and you've perfected the art of human 'doings' very well, but when it comes to emotional intelligence and the art of living and being, you don't half make it hard work sometimes.

Feeling flustered

"Oh, my goodness we're late, Louie. I wish my life was like in the movies, all birds singing and music playing, wandering through the fields, and enjoying picnics in the sunshine, laughing with friends. Maybe one day or maybe never. Let's go! I've no time for make-up."

Wow, she's running down the stairs, maybe she's finally embracing a moment with no make-up! It's looking even better - she now has my collar and lead, yippee! We're off for a walk, we're off for a walk, I sing to myself as I dance around the kitchen tip toeing from one foot to the other, completely unable to contain my excitement. It's the small moments that really matter.

"Louie, sit still whilst I put your collar on, we're already late."

Chill, mum! Late for what? Why are you always on a schedule? Can't we just walk and not clock-watch? You humans invented watches and you've forgotten how to be. I can tell you as a dog I just know when it's dinner time and sometimes I even have to remind you! For humans that are so clever, it never ceases to amaze me that you have often disconnected from your own intuition and circadian rhythm.

As we leave the house, the air is fresh. Mum looks amazing as we jog down the road, with a glow in her cheeks, all natural with no make-up. Don't get me wrong, she looks pretty with make-up too but either way, I think she's beautiful. Her beauty shines through her eyes. I'm so happy... oh wait, oh no, I think this is the way to the groomers. Yikes! Time to start applying the brakes. Maybe, if I water a few more bushes and delay her, we'll miss the appointment. You see, I don't dislike the groomers, I see a very nice lady who cuddles me and gives me biscuits, but I just don't like the deodorant she sprays on me afterwards. I mean, how am I supposed to blend in and avoid predators if I smell like potpourri?

"I'll be back in an hour to collect him." Mum said to my groomer as she left me. Yes, she left me! Exposed on the grooming table. Well, there's only one thing to do, embrace it. I'm sure I'll find something to enjoy in my hour of so-called pampering.

An hour later, the door went and in walked mum. I was feeling quite smug. I knew what was coming next.

"I forgot to clean Louie's teeth last time, so I did them this time and to apologise, I added a little facial for him."

Ha! Mum's jaw dropped.

"A facial? Do dogs even have facials? When can I book in?" said mum, looking at me as I sat wagging my tail all relaxed.

As mum paid, the groomer handed her a leaflet for a course called 'Broadband Consciousness' and said it was worth looking into. Mum looked completely distracted and as she bent down to tie her shoelace, she popped the leaflet down on the sideboard.

As we left, mum asked, "Did she really give you a facial?" Mum thought she was talking to herself, but little did she realise, I understood every word. Yes, she did give me a facial, and I loved every second of it, my eyes smugly told her. I can always find something good in a situation I'm not so fond of. I focussed on the facial rather than the noisy clippers because that makes me feel better. Do you focus on the positives in situations? Can you always seek them out?

After the groomers, mum always takes me for a walk. On this occasion, she was very quiet and looked completely distracted. She was missing the birds flying by, people saying hello and smiling at her, and she looked lost, distant and unhappy. She spends far too much time in her head thinking, rather than in her heart and just being, but I knew that she would be happier when we got back to Lola's. Lola always makes mum laugh. I just wish that she could be her 'happy self' more often. Life is for living, isn't it?

"Oh shucks, Louie. I've left that leaflet at the groomers." What will she think of me? I could've at least had the decency to take it and then put it in the nearest bin."

Seriously mum, stop worrying about what people will think - and maybe just read the blooming leaflet rather than discarding everything that is in front of you?

Oooh the stream looks inviting today and I need to get this wretched perfume smell off me. Yes, she's deep in thought, I'm sure I can make a run for it now... there are some advantages to her not being present.

"Louie, come back, no, no, no, no, Louie stop!"

EEK – I think she's clocked me. I know she tells people that I pretend to be deaf and yup, this is going to be one of those moments. I tip toe into the water; I don't like it when I can't touch the floor so brooks are perfect for me. I lay down and feel the fresh stream of water flow over me. This is what life is about, appreciating the small things, listening to the flow of water around me and being grateful for fresh water to drink and to bathe away unwanted perfume smells.

"Louie, seriously. You've just been groomed and now you're going to stink. Why can't you at least stay clean for a few days whilst we're staying at Lola's house?"

Oh dear. I think I'm in the doghouse again, but on the bright side, Lola will cheer her up.

We arrived back at Lola's and Bella came to the door to greet us. Everyone approved of my haircut and I'm sure Bella was envious of my facial.

Glimpses of reality

Later that evening, mum and Lola cracked open the wine and sat by the log burner, flames ablaze. The heat and cosiness were a perfect end to a perfect day. Aw no, please mum, don't tell that story again.

"Hey Lola, do you remember when we first met walking and Louie took a shine to Bella, I've never seen him so lovesick. That morning when we got home, he left his breakfast untouched and sat at the top of the stairs howling. I cried with laughter, even Jim was amused, I've never seen anything like it."

Seriously mum, it wasn't funny and why did you have to embarrass me? Bella and I are strictly friends. We sat in silence for the next few minutes, the atmosphere was more sombre, almost reflective.

"How was your day Ellen, how are you feeling about things now? You've had some pretty major life transitions recently." said Lola.

"Do you know Lola, you're right. I feel a little lost, I just don't know anymore, I feel like life wasn't meant to be like this. I thought I would be living, happy ever after. Instead, I just feel a little bit like I'm on a treadmill and life is passing me by. I'm always trying to be someone I'm not, trying to fit in and please people, it's exhausting!"

"Hey Ellen, I keep forgetting to tell you... there is this event local to us, and I think it is just what the doctor ordered. I know it will be inspiring. It's a recharge day, by Broadband Consciousness and they are amazing at what they do. I've heard so many people rave about this. Shall we go?"

Ha! As if by coincidence (or the universe at work,) the course had cropped back up again - she couldn't get away with leaving that leaflet behind. I'm a firm believer that 'what is for you, won't go by you' and it was clearly a sign. Maybe this is the next part of her journey. Maybe Bella and I can have an afternoon to ourselves, free of coaching duties and able to sleep in peace whilst they go off on a jaunt.

"The great thing is Ellen; dogs are allowed at the venue so Lord Louie and Bella can come."

Oh, dear Lord! Lord Louie indeed. There was me thinking I'd get a day off. Mum is always looking for dog friendly venues and there is no way she will go without me.

Several hours later, I was woken from a deep slumber by the crackling of the log burner and the laughter and joy in the room. It was the perfect energy to relax and curl up. Mum's cheeks were rosy from the glow of the fire, or the wine. Whichever, she looked happy and a sparkle in her eye told me she had experienced another wonderful evening with her friend. It was my 'real' mum back, I don't get to see her true happiness often, and it always seems more accidental than deliberate. Maybe one day she will live deliberately, rather than accidentally. She's far happier and her life seems so much more effortless when she's being herself.

This is the reality; this is the real her. If only she could see 'it' and be 'it' more often.

Recharge your batteries

My mum is disillusioned in thinking she's got to look after me. I've heard her tell all her friends that it's like having a 2-year-old, dependent forever. Yet she doesn't quite see it from my perspective.

I am on high alert 24/7. She says that parents of babies are sleep deprived but let me tell you, us earth angels have a huge responsibility to guard the house, protect our owners, listen out for potential intruders like the postman - why do they have to bang the letterbox so loud and scare the bejesus out of us or ring the doorbell when we're asleep? Not to mention being on high alert in case a human tries to escape without us noticing, I mean where do they even go for hours on end that they can't take us with them? In these moments I have temporarily lost my pack and I am now the sole defender of our home. Mum talks to her friends about double time and shift premiums but I don't see any extra sausages in my pay checks at month end.

Recharge day had arrived. "Where are our tickets for Recharge, Lola?" asked mum.

At that moment the ding-dong chime of the doorbell went. It was only 08:45. Oh my goodness, we're under attack again. I race to the window to investigate, being the man of the house and all.

But, today is different and I can chaperone her. Luckily the ding-dong was the postman delivering the tickets for today. How timely. Thank you, universe. Now that was definitely cutting it fine. It was obviously meant to be!

As we arrive at the venue and enter the room, the energy is high. People are laughing and giving each other hugs. Smiles all around. This feels a little different to other personal development events I've had the pleasure of chaperoning mum to over the years. There haven't been many, but she's dabbled in the past and never taken it any further. Accidentally through work she's attended resilience courses for accountants. It's hardly that a spreadsheet is going to hurt her feelings, is it now? They were useful, but she found the learning accrued at these events never really stuck.

I can see the relief on mum's face when we were invited to take our seats. She looks a bit overwhelmed, and I heard her saying to

Lola that she felt a bit awkward when everyone was greeting her with a hug. It is such a British reaction to maintain a stiff upper lip and that affection is only for people you know, and only then if you're female. Men can only shake hands, unless of course they're Italian and then it's perfectly acceptable for another man to kiss you on the cheek. Rules, rules, rules of society! You humans have created some strange ones and what is even more comical is that you allow them to dictate what you can and can't do. Funny how you think you live in a democracy, yet your minds are sometimes the least democratic of them all.

Back to the event, I look up and there is an energised man, centre stage, who is wearing a fancy patterned jacket. He introduces himself as the Minister of Inspiration. I like him, I hope mum does too! He seems different and full of life. Now, that's a dose of medicine mum could do with.

He speaks so eloquently and his message is so clear. "My life is not perfect externally, but I am not waiting to be happy," declares the minister. I cannot contain myself; all my wishes are coming true. Another earth angel giving people more tools for living. I've been trying to communicate this message to mum for years and finally I've found a human for her to hear these words from. He has actually told my mum that happiness is an inside job. I can see her looking confused. She whispers to Lola, that it's alright for him but how could it possibly work for her?

As if by the magic of the universe, he got the message of her whisper and responded.

"You're probably sitting there thinking that it's alright for me, and it is, but it can be for you too. I'm going to share with you how. How to be happy even though you've not got your perfect home yet, haven't found the right partner yet, or perhaps feel unfulfilled in your job".

Mum shuffled in her seat, looking uneasy as if he was speaking to her and her only. It's not voodoo and he may not be psychic, but he understands humans just as I do - how that magical piece of kit in your head, also known as your brain, can either be your ticket to a fulfilled life or a barricade that imprisons you.

Sizzling sausages

The minister went on to share part of the 'how' and demonstrated this with fun, humour, and energy with a sausage machine concept.

I chuckle to myself and think, I knew there was a reason why I loved sausages so much. Not only do they taste amazing, but the machine shows you how to create a fulfilled life. Now we're talking!

As the minister puts on his apron that has writing scribed 'prick with a fork' and a picture of sausages, he starts laughing, the audience laughing with him. The energy is infectious and it is clear that the fun is being shared with like-'hearted' people. He uses a table as a prop for a sausage machine and begins to introduce the concept of 'what we put in we get out'.

This is how most humans live, they are waiting at the end of the sausage machine for external things to show up in their lives to release an internal feeling. Well, the minister explains it very succinctly. He calls these humans the 'waiters' in society, constantly waiting for good to come along, just like that lottery win. Sadly, for many, they wait their whole life, accidentally experiencing ups, yet not truly living deliberately. The ingredients going in the sausage machine include all the wrong feelings, doubt, worry, stress, anxiety, frustration and the list goes on. Yet, the humans are waiting at the other end of the sausage machine expecting happiness, joy, contentment, fulfilment, even though all they are putting in is stress and worry. It just backs up my theory that whilst the human race is highly intelligent, you don't often make it hard work for yourselves to be emotionally intelligent.

The minister goes on to explain that how to live a happy life, lies in becoming a creator by moving to the front end of the sausage machine and putting the ingredients, the feelings into the sausage machine rather than waiting for the events to give you permission to release them. After all, we own all the amazing feelings, we have just forgotten how to release them.

Sausage machine and slippers

I play this wonderful game with mum and it's a great example of the sausage machine in action.

Often, when she and Lola leave the house, I go around investigating to see how I can best plan my free time and relocate mum's objects. First of all, I have to complete the discovery phase. What had she left out for me to hide? A pair of high heeled shoes in the utility room. Oh, dear, they do bring back memories of when I was just a small boy. I temporarily feel a little guilty now that I am older and wiser, but I did have a thing for chewing her shoes. Many of her favourite pairs emigrated to shoe heaven because of me. On the positive side though, she got to buy some more, so I probably did her a favour. Let's go with that thought, it serves me and my feelings better.

One fateful day, she'd hung all her washing out on a clothes horse, albeit a metal rack that makes some loud scary noises when it slides down the wall and crashes to the floor, it doesn't half make me jump, but that day, it stood out in its full glory, undergarments and socks hanging low enough for me to cherry pick from the bottom rung.

Several hours later, I'd had a lovely afternoon and was feeling quite pleased with myself. The generous next-door neighbour had visited with a special treat for mum and Lola. Some free-range eggs which he had placed on the side in the kitchen. I thought they'd be pleased as they were running low, and of course Bella and I got biscuits. He looks after us and often plays ball with us in the garden if our humans are out.

As I drifted off into a slumber, curled up on the chair in the window next to Bella, I heard a car outside. Yay, mum was home first. I hoped she'd be pleased with my efforts that day; they usually make her smile. As the key turned in the door, I rushed to greet her and help her carry her belongings in. As she had nothing to give me, I rustled through her handbag as she placed it down on the floor. Ooh a purse! That was perfect. I collected the purse in my mouth and trotted through to the living room, unable to contain my excitement from having a fun filled day. Putting fun in the sausage machine and coupled with the fact that mum was home, I was super excited to see what she thought of my efforts. I pranced around the living room, eyes half closed, crying with excitement. Those little moments are what create and make life and its memories.

"Oh Louie, you have been busy today." she stated as she tiptoed across the floor, avoiding the bright pink sock and various other undergarments I'd carefully placed throughout the house, not to mention the bright pink boot slipper with stars that I'd placed on the window sill.

I heard mum laugh out loud as she spotted the pink slipper in the window. "Louie, you are one crazy kid."

Mum, I'm a dog not a baby goat, I laughed back with her. This is what life is about, creating fun and happiness and joy.

"Louie, let's see what else you've been up to whilst I've been gone," she said as she rounded the corner to explore upstairs. First, she'd found a high-heeled boot on her bed. I was proud of that one, her long knee-high boots are quite heavy to heave up onto the bed. The timing of the jump is pertinent. This was coupled along with her law of attraction book which I had been reviewing. I mean seriously guys, this stuff works. All you need is imagination, belief, and to know how to use the sausage machine correctly. In the next room she'd found my squeaky ball on the spare bed along with one of Lola's slippers.

She sat down on the bed to cuddle me, laugh, and tell me what a funny boy I was. Why thank you mum, I was so pleased I had created some laughter that day.

As we returned back down the stairs, mum was joyous and smiling, the sausage machine was really working. Until... aw no, she'd clocked the eggs on the side and the penny had dropped. Instantly I saw her change, her body language, thoughts and feelings. She went bright red as the words tumbled out of her mouth.

"Louie, Tony has been in and has seen my underwear?" Whoops, I was hoping she hadn't noticed that bit. In an instant, the sausage machine ingredients had changed from joy and laughter to embarrassment and panic. If only there, in that moment, she realised that she had switched the batch of sausages she was creating. Oh dear. One day, she'll get it.

Do you create fun?

Back to recharge day and the minister on the stage. I hope I didn't miss anything important.

Deepening eloquence

The message we were given by the minister was so clear and precise, I could see that it really hit home to mum's heart, visibly waking up her senses. There was so much truth in the stories and the need to be, keeping up with the Joneses and the pressure we put on ourselves to have the big house, big car, big job and yet when we get the big house, big car, big job, there is always a bigger house, car or job to be had.

Chasing that pot of gold at the end of the rainbow and always feeling pressure and therefore putting more pressure into the sausage machine. For goodness' sake, it's not a pressure cooker.

The message I took away from the day is that eloquent messages are always around us, if we are open to them. Opening ourselves up to learning, can only lead to an enhancement of our lives. If we are open to the whispers from people, nudges from the universe, or whatever you believe in, there are signs and guidance always around that are inviting you to step further into living your life!

Later that day, as we left, there was a sign-up sheet by the door for a full course. Mum walked out the door and my heart sank; I knew this was a piece of the puzzle for her happiness. The vision board had been great but without self-love and belief it would always require more effort.

However, something within her changed at that point, and as we reached the main entrance, mum stopped in her tracks and called out to Lola. "Wait up, can you take Lord Louie for one moment, there's something I must do!"

Several weeks later, my bra is fitted firmly back on. This means only one thing… you guessed it, a trip in the car. Today is a special day, for it's the start of a new chapter. Mum did run back and sign up for the course and today is the very first day of an exciting week. And guess what? It's a dog friendly venue. Although, I'm not sure if this is a good or bad thing yet. The jury's still out.

As we arrived at the venue, the air was fresh and the birds were tweeting. There was an excitable energy all around. It reminded me of spring. It was a time for renewal and growth, and I was extremely excited for mum's next chapter.

Glimmer of light

As we sat in the venue, the Minister of Inspiration and his wonderful partner Elizabeth, shone their brightness on the participants. They invited participants to share their stories with the group and learn how their stories were mostly untrue, unfounded beliefs and opinions about themselves. Perception isn't always reality, is it?

Over the next few days, I sat and listened, truly listened, and for the first time, I saw my real mum start to shine, consistently and deliberately, not accidentally. Now you know why her email address is shine@lisavictoria.co.uk because she wants to share all her gifts to help others shine bright too.

As she told her story my heart sank. This wasn't the person that I saw sat in front of me, my wonderful mum who I could truly see. Yet, I was starting to learn why she didn't value herself and why she experiences such low energy feelings which stop her from truly living.

Accidental programming

Mum learned a lot about herself that week and about why we think, feel and do things that perhaps don't serve us, or the people around us. She learned that humans have been accidentally programmed and that they never challenge this programming. You humans are all born equal and then life happens to you. You become puppets and start to conform to rules based on what society says you should and shouldn't do. For example, what your parents, peers or teachers say you should and shouldn't do. This leads to programmed thoughts, values and behaviours, and to add to this, things you learn through observation based on how people react in certain situations also become part of the programming.

Road rage is a great example. The most sensible of people go completely bonkers and out of character if something doesn't go their way on the road. Take for example a scenario where you witness someone cutting someone you know up. How many times have you witnessed them turn into a monster, a version of them that isn't really them? You hear me? You know exactly what I'm talking about, I'm sure you've seen it yourselves. I certainly have whilst being strapped into the back seat in my bra in the car. Ha-ha, that rhymes. I can be quite funny sometimes. Anyway, that's what mum discovered about accidental programming. She also learned that the audio version is in her head, like a generator, waiting to respond with a default answer. Boy! Have I seen this and heard the words come out of her mouth about not enjoying her job, blah, blah, blah? I won't even use up my energy repeating it.

This was another piece to her puzzle of life. A real light bulb moment. Up to that point she had never considered her default programming. She just thought that life happened to her and that she had no control over her response. It was just who she was, and that she simply couldn't change. Listening to what was said during the course, I could see mum's thinking start to change. Maybe she did have a say in her life, and maybe she could change her response. Bingo! It's not that I've been trying to tell her this with the angels, like, since forever! Humph!

Inner rainbows

I always find it fascinating when mum stops to look at a rainbow. It may be dark, grey, and raining all around, but she always focuses on the vibrant colours in the sky and not the rest which is gloomy. I wish she did this with her life too, because there is always something good to find if you choose to focus your attention on the rainbows in your life.

Mum was having a conversation with another lady in the group. Her excitement and newfound lease of thoughts were strongly shining through. She said, "Wow! I remember learning to drive and not having clutch control, revving the engine, having to look where my gear stick was and where my pedals were to change gears. Now, I can drive for miles and not even know how I got there. I am talented and clever after all."

Erm… jeez mum! You never told me you were driving in a semi-conscious state. I'm actually quite thankful for my 'bra in the car' now!

Mum was starting to question everything that was in her subconscious programming and sift through what served her and what didn't, coming up with different ways to think and feel in different situations. Most importantly, she was learning to love and appreciate herself. It was clear she was finding her inner shards of colour, reflecting the torch light within, just like a rainbow and creating a beautiful external view. She looked even more radiant and beautiful with an inner light of confidence. Yes! Mum is on a full rainbow beam. It was spectacular to see!

Accidental programmed 'funnies'

As mum discovered who she was not, she realised she now had the freedom to be who she truly is in her heart. Some of her outdated beliefs were crazy. Here are some of the things I learned about my mum and indeed about other people in the group that week.

"I can't possibly go out of the house to get a pint of milk without make-up on. Even though it's 10pm and the shop is literally around the corner, it's dark and no one will see, but what if I bump into someone I know? Heaven forbid they'll judge me."

Jeez! You humans worry so much about what people think that you'll spend half an hour putting make-up on just to go and get a pint of milk?! Seriously!

"I don't want to go to the gym tonight, I'm far too tired. I've had a busy day at work and I just need to rest, I'll catch the 8 o'clock spin session next week. At precisely 8pm, the thoughts change to, why didn't I go to the gym tonight? I'm lazy and now I feel like I'm missing out."

Sound familiar? I don't even know why you go to the gym. I prefer running across the fields and getting fresh air but each to their own, I guess.

More and more thoughts and experiences came rattling out from around the room:

"I need to prove myself because society says blondes are dumb. This makes me feel under immense amounts of pressure to conform to society norms and doesn't allow me to be me."

Eye roll. Yes! Mum is blonde and it took her a degree and qualifying as an accountant to realise that she didn't need to prove anything to anyone. How freeing!

"Don't get up and dance, everyone will laugh at you."

Did you ever hear a two- or three-year-old say that? Never! They're too busy having FUN!

"I feel trapped in my job, I can't possibly leave, I've made my bed and I must lie in it."

Well shoot me now. How many people do you think have career changes? Yes, lots! Nothing is permanent. If you don't like it, or you're running out of money, there are always options. Countless options, if you believe.

Just being

Several weeks after the course, we were walking to our local café in Towcester. It's a wonderful market town, steeped in history. The original A road from London runs straight through the middle of it and historically, Charles Dickens would rest at the Saracen's head on his way through. I just love learning new things, and it's so exciting that we get to live in a town where Dickens would visit.

When we first moved here, I remember mum having to spell out our address over the phone. T O W C E S T E R. Not like a toaster that you put bread in. It sounds like it, but it isn't spelled like it. And mum thought moving away from Wales with places like 'Llanfairpwllgwyngyllgogerychwyrndrobwllllantysiliogogogoch' would make it easier to spell her address. Hah! I think the universe is just teasing her. She loves it, really. If you think that place in Wales isn't real, I can assure you it is. Mum has even made me pose for a photo outside the train station. Although, you can barely tell it's me because she's stood so far away just to get the whole name of the town in. Fun times.

At the café, I sit and I watch, and I listen. As I observe, most humans are head down in their phones, the minute your companion leaves the table or before they arrive, people can't help themselves, they just pull out their mobile devices and they scroll, and they scroll, and they scroll. What happened to the other senses? Smell, and peripheral vision, interacting and smiling with another human being, patting a nearby dog (ahem), maybe me? Let's face it, we all love a pat on the back.

I was once on the train with mum when we played this game where I sat in the aisle and refused to move until the person wanting to pass gave me a cuddle. You can quite quickly suss out the stressed humans or the kind ones. It was part of my research for this book. Did you know stroking a dog, releases happy hormones? The people that stroked me were working from their hearts - I could see the joy in their eyes and they were definitely in the moment, whereas the people who were in their heads, looked stressed and distant. I felt sad for them, for the simple fact that they were missing the joy of a moment.

Back to the coffee aka herbal tea. Lola and mum were chatting and laughing. It was great to see them both in the moment, relaxed and nowhere to go, no to do list to worry about, just friends enjoying a simple coffee.

The next chapter

"Hey Ellen, I forgot to mention, there is a great event in London soon with Lorna Byrne and Mike Dooley. It's an event to learn how to connect with your angels and it's in three weeks' time. Are you up for it?"

"I'm not sure. I don't even know who Lorna is. But Mike Dooley's course is on my vision board, and I do love the law of attraction concept."

Lola went on to explain that Lorna Byrne was famous for connecting with angels and showing people how they too can connect with theirs for guidance and support.

"I'm still not sure. As much as I would love to, I think that's the date I exchange on my house." mum said.

"Well, we can always pull out if your house goes through, it's only £30," said Lola.

"Very true, let's do it!"

Right there in the coffee shop, the tickets were booked. Isn't technology fascinating, so long as you humans are using it as a tool and not letting the tool hypnotise you. I hope these tickets arrive slightly earlier than the Broadband Consciousness tickets. Talk about the universe cutting it fine. However, it did deliver in the end. This is the magical thing about the universe, the flow may not always be in line with your expected timing, but it always has a way of working itself out. 'What's meant for you won't pass you by', as the saying goes!

Yay! I can feel another trip on the train coming up. Last time it was Edinburgh, this time it's London. Maybe I'll get to see the Queen of England!

They finished their drinks. "Come on – let's go home," said mum, "It's Louie's birthday tomorrow, I'm going to bake us a cake to celebrate and we can have a party, just the four of us."

Discovering you

Later that afternoon we were all in the kitchen and baking, ingredients spread all over the counter top. I loved how she was starting to reignite her passions for things she hadn't done for a while. She had always baked basic cakes, but since she was growing in confidence and exploring her creative side, she had discovered that she was not just an accountant but also a creative being with many skills. Who would've guessed she'd be singing along to music, relighting her passion for dancing and translating that into an afternoon of baking and modelling out of icing? She was lost for hours, perfecting models of people and a very impressive version of me too! I loved watching her at that moment. Happy and content, releasing her creative side and embracing her true self creating a masterpiece of a cake for her friends and family. I'm proud of the human she was unbecoming. Finally, discovering and letting her true self come to the surface.

Her masterpiece was finished. She proudly took some pictures to share, something she would never have done before. As she loaded Facebook, she accidentally came across the pink wellington boots picture. She hesitated for a moment and I could read her thoughts. Go on, do it! I dare you. At that moment she clicked 'post'. There! The picture was on Facebook, shining in her natural beauty, no longer worrying about what people would think of her, along with the cake and my model version of me!

LORD LOUIE'S LESSONS

1. Do you feel like there is something missing in your life? What feeling are you searching for?
2. What body language signals do you think you give off to others around you? Confidence, being closed off, or withdrawn? Does this change from situation to situation?
3. What do you see through your blackened lenses? If you could swap them for rainbow lenses, what might you see?
4. What accidental programming do you have that no longer serves you? Can you spot any common themes? Can you learn to laugh at things that you no longer value? What has been internalised as a truth which is just an outdated opinion? Please sit and take time to reflect on this. It will help you shift some blocks and be able to move forwards with ease and grace.

If you haven't done so already, don't forget to download your complimentary workbook with Lord Louie's questions from the end of each chapter, to support your own self-discovery. There really is huge value in writing things down instead of just 'thinking' them through.

You can get your workbook here:
heartvoice.co.uk/behappynow

Oh, and if you'd like to see the pictures mentioned in this chapter, then head over to our Facebook group, we'd love to share these memories with you. Click here to join our Facebook group (Lead with the Heart - https://www.facebook.com/groups/leadwiththeheart)

Discovery — Finding You

Discover your heart
It's where the truth is
The thoughts that pass
Are none of your biz?

Often, we think
But we forget to feel
Caught up in the thoughts
So often not real

Notice what's around you
Take a moment, just be
Lots to be thankful for
Gratitude will set you free

For when we are thankful
We focus on what we've got
The negative voice quietened
That say's, we've not got a lot

We've more than we think
Just look around and see
Memories, things, and life
That's a big one to me

For waking up this morn
Is all that we need
The gift of life itself
Our day is what we feed

Nurture the right thoughts
Take steps, and show up
Trust in universal magic
To fill up life's cup

In our heart, lays the truth
Our guidance we can hear
Just sit still, and listen
Little whispers, in your ear

Discover your voice
Your passion within
Right there in your heart
Start living, just begin

Chapter 5

DISCOVERY – A UNIVERSAL ENERGY

'the process of finding information, a place, or
an object, especially for the first time'

Cambridge Dictionary

A new abode

It was the day of the move. Mum hadn't procured a lot of material possessions so she hired a local van to move us in and it couldn't have been brighter. Lola and mum laughed as the orange clapped out van rounded the corner, pop popping up the road. With a few select items of furniture, a bed, a cuddle chair, plants, a microwave, along with her clothes and not much more, the van was loaded and we were off. A new chapter was beginning. That's one thing she's learnt about life; the only constant is change and there are two ways she can approach this. Embrace it or crumble! Luckily she's putting her 'big girl pants' on today and is embracing the change. I can tell because they are laughing about the van. The old her would worry about it getting to the other side of town. It's not like we're moving far, We're just a short walk from Lola and Bella.

The van pulled up on our new drive and we pulled up next to it, Lola and Bella in convoy behind. There was no way she was going to let mum do this alone. What a great best friend!

The workmen unloaded mum's limited possessions. The house felt a little sparse with one cuddle chair in the middle of the living room, but it was her home. No one could take that away from her. She'd been chattering to me as she does. As we had approached this day there were mixed emotions of excitement and fear of having the responsibility of a mortgage. I knew she would be just fine. Especially as she was now growing in confidence.

This was her time to start spreading her own wings, learning and discovering how to get comfortable in her own company. How to create a relationship with herself and learn to enjoy being alone. With me of course she wasn't truly alone, but I'm referring to when other humans aren't around. Often humans are fearful of being alone and have this fear of missing out.

She was learning to trust in her own ability and not be so dependent on others for happiness. She placed some positive affirmations by the front door, her pink rose quartz crystal by the bed, her vision board in the study, and a beautiful crystal prism was placed on the windowsill in the living room catching the light and reflecting a rainbow across the whole room. It goes without saying that she had the wine glasses to hand, ready for the evening ahead with Lola.

Once the van had been unpacked, Lola and Bella disappeared for the afternoon to do their errands. Mum and I sat on the cuddle chair.

"This is it, Louie. This is our new life. Do you think we will be okay?"

I knew we would be. Just as we always had been.

That evening, you could see the relief on her face as Lola and Bella came in. She's never lived on her own before. This was a big deal, and one I knew was going to stretch her out of her comfort zone. Thank goodness for friends and wine. At least tonight she would be in good company!

The wine flowed, they laughed and ate takeaway out of the box. We still had a lot to buy to fill the place, but material things do not equate to happiness. I could see it right there on her face as Lola said how proud she must be to have made such a big step. Mum blushed but I could tell that secretly she was proud too. They were both present, right there in the moment, sat on the floor. They could have been sitting in a mansion but friendship and laughter is a moment thing, not a material thing.

It was time for Bella and Lola to walk home.

"You'll be just fine, but call me if you need anything and I'll be right back," Lola promised.

As mum hugged Lola and closed the door a little tear rolled down her cheek.

Freedom to choose

The next morning mum stirred and smiled. I had been watching tentatively for the past hour so I could gauge her response to waking up in her first ever home. It was positive. She was smiling.

"Louie, we survived the night on our own." Relief and excitement written all over her face, as if she had achieved something. Well, she had and she was starting to feel it, and not just the achievement of owning a home, a material thing, we're talking achievement of self-belief. She can do this!

A new found freedom had been presented to mum. After several weeks and lots of trips to the shops, she was creating her space and our home. I could see she was enjoying it, embracing the change as opposed to resisting it.

Lola had been over with Bella to help mum settle in, but they couldn't be here all the time and it was the first dreaded Friday evening where Lola couldn't come over. Mum was moaning that she felt like she was missing out, mainly because she thought that either all the single people were out having fun and other couples were at home all loved up. She was playing this fantastical story in her mind that simply wasn't a reality for everyone. Then something clicked. She simply said, if she had to be at home on a Friday night she might as well make the most of it. This was a huge shift in her perspective. She ordered a takeaway, opened some wine and put on her favourite music. Who says you can't have a party for one? Do you put your favourite music on often enough?

Mum was in the process of discovering who she was and that she actually enjoyed her own company and of course, it goes without saying, mine too! She was starting to discover who she was and what she is actually capable of when she stepped outside of her comfort zone. A single life, living on her own wasn't as bad as she thought.

As we climbed into bed that evening, mum wished me good-night, as she always does and spoke. "Do you know, Louie, I'm actually enjoying having our own space, it's quite liberating." Now that was a shift.

Penguin perfection

It was a cold snowy day, on the weekend of our trip to London, and the event with Mike Dooley and Lorna Byrne. We met Lola and Bella on the platform.

Mum insisted that I wore my penguin jumper to keep me warm. I was getting more adoring looks than normal and lapped up the attention. I love engaging with people, I get to bring joy to their day by wagging my tail and smiling too. It always baffles me as to why humans often shy away from attention and compliments, denying another the pleasure of giving you a compliment or a smile, which all you have to do is simply return. Most often, I see you trying to fit in and not stand out. I've certainly heard many conversations with mum and her people about getting it right. Not being too out there, or putting your head above the parapet in case anyone shoots you down in flames. Yet she sticks me in a penguin jumper! How unique do I look now? But I embrace my individuality and in return I get smiles and cuddles.

What's not to like? If only you humans would wear your 'penguin' outfits more often and engage with more people. The only time you might think this is remotely acceptable is at Christmas when there appears to be a competition for the most outrageous jumper. You have fun, you laugh, goodness forbid you engage with others, being in the moment and not worrying about what others think because you're having fun.

"Hey Lola, have you ever travelled first class on a train, that would be fun, wouldn't it? Sometime."

"Yes, but maybe not today with the tickets we have."

All aboard

As we boarded the train we squeezed into a seat, the only one we could find. We had lost Lola and Bella in the crowd getting onto the train. Mum temporarily started to panic and then said to me, "It's okay Louie, we'll find them, I know." Finally, she's starting to wake up, calmer, and more rational thoughts.

As the train pulled into the next station, a gentleman boarded. He sat next to mum in the aisle seat blocking her in. As mum glanced around the carriage shuffling me between her feet to make room, I saw her clock the sign that said, first class. Oh dear, here we go again, the rollercoaster of thoughts and emotions, one minute feeling like she's got this, the next in a blind panic of worry. I can tell because her breath quickens and she looks anxious. You may often think you can hide your feelings but really you can't. Here we go again, just breathe and think rationally mum! I'm back in coaching mode again and as if by magic, she's now tapped into my unspoken words. She softens, I can see her thoughts changing, and she's starting to manage them.

The train attendant announces over the tannoy, "due to the volume of passengers on this train today, we're downgrading first class and opening it up to all passengers, all first-class ticket holders will get a refund."

The edges of mum's lips start to turn up, a smile appearing on her face. I can read her like a book, she visualised sitting in first class, accidentally ended up there, momentarily panicked and then realised what she's manifested. Thoughts often create our reality, and we ought to mind them wisely.

The gentleman next to mum keeps smiling at me, and asks mum if he can say hello. It's human etiquette with fur babies, always ask first because some of us are more scared than others. They get chatting as I lap up the attention once more. I love our adventures. I learn so much from the people we meet and observing their behaviours. As they chatted, it became apparent that this gentleman was in a panto, mum still had no clue who he was, she's very naïve sometimes. I chuckle to myself at her innocence, it's very endearing.

As soon as the train pulled into Euston, the gentleman said his goodbyes. Mum quickly grabbed her phone out and googled 'panto London' to see who she had been talking to. She noticed it was 11:33 on her phone. She had no clue that this was a signpost that the angels were with her and she was on the right path. Maybe one day I'll deliver the message of significance in numbers.

"Ellen, there you are," came Lola's voice, "we lost you."

"You'll never guess what just happened Lola," mum's voice was full of excitement. "We just sat next to someone famous, he was lovely and so well grounded, it was such a delightful conversation."

"Who was it?" asked Lola excitedly.

"I've no idea."

Oh dear, she was never up on famous people.

We moved through the station. It was so busy, people rushing here, there, and everywhere. Astonishing to see a group of grown adults, staring at the boards, awaiting the announcement of the platform for their train. As soon as it did flash up, it was like a race. Etiquette and manners out of the window as people pushed and ran towards the platform number as if their life depended on it. Stress and fear strewn across their faces. I don't like it all that much.

Underground daffodils

As we approached the escalator, mum scooped me up in her arms, as did Lola with Bella. Apparently, dogs are only allowed on escalators in London if they are being carried. My mum is strong but by goodness, it's a good job I'm an earth angel in disguise as a Spaniel and not a 30 kilo Alsatian; now that would be interesting, I chuckle to myself. The mad rush continues on the escalator as we stand in very British fashion, lined up on the left.

The London underground is a very interesting place. People leap onto carriages as the doors beep when they're closing, some win, some are defeated. Sweat pours off their brows just to catch a train, even though the next one is usually only a couple of minutes away.

I liken these humans to underground daffodils. When a daffodil bulb is planted, it cannot see the beauty of the blue skies and colourful flowers that surround it, all it can see is darkness. Yet when the bulb grows and breaks through the soil, it can start to see how different the world looks. Some humans are merely bulbs that cannot see the beauty yet. Whilst others trust the process and grow, and that's when life comes into colour, just like a daffodil. I hope you can see the beauty around you.

As mum holds me in her arms, the train starts to pull away. Ouch, my ears! What on earth is that screeching, surely, they'd do well to oil the tracks? We don't really need to hold on to the hand rails. The carriage is so packed, we're all standing upright, like sardines packed tightly together. Not a glance shared or a smile for that matter. So close physically, yet so distant emotionally. It must be the good old British stiff upper lip again.

As the train comes to an abrupt halt several stops later, the doors slide open. We have arrived at Angel station. How purposeful, given we are having a day out with the Angels. So far so good, the universe is aligning.

Ascending

As we alight the staircase and come back into the fresh air, Lola has to grab mum and steer her. She's about to bump into the back of a chap wearing a number 33 rugby shirt. How apt, the same number presenting itself again, and yet she's still clueless. It's practically hitting her in the face and she cannot see it. I think I need a holiday!

After apologising to the handsome chap, she nearly bumped into, mum catches her feet and her breath and then starts talking excitedly and rapidly, "Lola, I've been desperate to share something with you. I can't believe we got split up on the train. Something really strange happened last night."

"Calm down Ellen, you're very excitable. Just breathe and tell me."

"Okay, I just had an extraordinary experience. After knowing we were coming to this event, I wanted to understand a little more about Lorna Byrne. I know of Mike Dooley from some friends but not much of Lorna."

"Where's this going?" said Lola.

"Well, this is where it gets really interesting..." Mum paused and smiled, keeping Lola in suspense.

"Tell me, tell me, tell me. What did you do?"

Mum went on to explain that as we put on our pyjamas last night and settled in for the evening, she googled Mike Dooley and Lorna Byrne and found a YouTube clip that she watched. In the video, Lorna invited the viewer, in this case, mum, to connect with her angels and see what message they had for her.

"Within ten minutes Lola, I had literally sketched out a book, 'Be Happy Now' as part of the Chasing Rainbows series. The angels said it was to be written through the eyes of Louie. How cool is that?! I doubt I'll be able to do it though, I've never written a book before and I was actually better at maths at school. English never was my forte."

Whaaaaaaaat?! No one told me I signed up for this when I adopted you as my mum. First, I have to coach you and now you want me to become an author. When will I get a day off? Maybe I need to book a retreat in Wales!

"Oh, my goodness Ellen, that's huge. I can't believe you're telling me this just as we're about to enter a talk. We have to explore this more later."

As we entered the room, there was a feeling of high energy, just like the time we were at Recharge Day. People were friendly and they seemed really happy. Much happier than our encounter on the underground. I wonder if people automatically default to being an underground daffodil on the underground - ha-ha, literally and theoretically definitely underground. Or, do different types of people hang out here? Regardless, this looked like it was going to be fun!

We climbed several steps up to our seats in the auditorium which created a 'U' shape to encircle the stage. Mum and Lola bumped into some of their other friends and they started to chat, embracing each other with big hugs and lots of laughter.

A vision of attraction

The moment arrived; Mike Dooley came out on stage with his contagious energy. Mum always spoke highly of him and I can agree that he does have a good energy. His words flowed, almost as if they were coming through him from the universe. With his American accent and words of wisdom on the Law of Attraction, the whole audience was hooked. All eyes glued to the stage.

"Thoughts become things," was his message. This is the universal Law of Attraction, whether they're good thoughts or bad, the universe responds, so make sure they're good and be careful what you wish for.

"Oh, my goodness," mum whispered to Lola, "what did I put on my vision board?"

Never mind what you put on your vision board, what you put in your mind is worrying sometimes. I can't keep up with your 70,000 or more, thoughts! You manifested first class on the train, but please be careful with your wand waving around in your head, it's currently got its 'L' plates on and is doing bunny hops down the road.

Several minutes later after people had shuffled in their seats, paying attention to Mike's every word, pens scribbling away capturing nuggets of inspiration, he welcomed Lorna Byrne to the stage.

An angelic presence

The energy in the room had shifted. Almost to a calmer, more serene and hypnotic energy. Lorna's Irish voice lilted in a lullaby way. I'm not sure I am going to last through a whole day without napping, I mean, I need my 18 hours of sleep, especially after the adventurous journey and nearly getting trodden on by number 33 man. For those of you that are curious, 33 is symbolic of being loved and blessed and that the angels are trying to catch your attention.

During the break, all the humans were buzzing with con-versations; the angels, the Law of Attraction, universal energy, God, the higher self, whatever they believed in that was bigger than them.

"What if we are connected to the universal Wi-Fi, just like our mobile phones. How is it that we can pick up a mobile that is not physically attached to anything and speak to a relative across the world and hear their voice? Maybe that's why, when I think of someone, they call several minutes or hours later after several months of no contact. Do you think I just Wi-Fi'd their energy?" said Lola.

Another bystander agreed, "Yes of course, that's exactly how it works. Equally, if you don't place your order with the universal Wi-Fi, then how long do you think it will take to appear?"

Everyone stood silent as the penny dropped. They'd either been ordering the wrong things with their thoughts, caught up in the reality of what was currently showing up in their lives, rather than what they wanted to show up. See for us four-legged earth angels, we magic this all the time, just like I magic sausages out of thin air!

Cosmic orders

I'll let you into my little secret as to how I do it:

I first create a clear vision on what I want, most crucially focusing on what I want, rather than what I don't want. Most humans focus on moaning about what's bad in their lives, which just attracts more of the same stuff, like a magnet. So, I ask for, and visualise sausages, not dog biscuits.

I connect with the universe and place my order. A bit like mum does with Amazon and let me tell you, she has that app on speed dial (quite literally) and we trust that our orders will be delivered. From Amazon, or the universe, we don't even entertain doubtful thoughts, we're steadfast in belief, knowing and certain. Then there's only one outcome that can possibly be, the thing we've ordered shows up into our conscious world, our current reality. Mum does this well with shopping but definitely still has her 'L' plates on with the universal shop of life. That's okay, we all have to start somewhere, just please pray for me that we have no accidents or bumps along the way!

So, the next thing I do is practice feeling grateful for my sausages in advance, I visualise what they will be like, what they will taste like, the ambiance around me. You've really got to get into the 'being state' as if it's already happened.

Then, I surrender the outcome and trust that one of my unemployed angels has run ahead and asked a human to help deliver the goods. I trust that the order is placed and it will be delivered. The Amazon man usually turns up too!

Lastly, I take away any expectations and trust in divine timing. I ordered sausages this morning, maybe I'll get them at lunch or maybe when we get home, but I trust that they will be delivered in the quickest and simplest way possible.

Guardian angel coaches

Throughout the day the audience participated in exercises to connect with their angels. We too have angels, just like you do, but you have a special angel, a 'guardian angel, often invisible to the naked eye, bodyguard, coach. guide, cheerleader, or non-judgmental friend. I thought I deserved a medal for my duties to mum, but hats off to her guardian angel, never leaving her side. At least I get my retreats in Wales. After a meditation exercise to meet your guardian angel, mum scribbled away in her notebook. I popped both paws on her knee to try and take a peek to see what hers was called. I could do with a direct dial to them for when I need a break. I felt blessed and grateful to know that mum had discovered my co-pilot, her guardian angel, to help steer this beautiful fledging human being. I wonder, what is their name?!

"Down Louie," she whispered as she gently slid my paws off her lap.

Shucks, I didn't get a name. Maybe one day if I listen carefully, I'll hear her talking to them. After all, she does talk a lot to herself, out loud! Mainly to beat herself up, but to give her credit, she does do this less now.

"Your angel's name is sacred to you and your angel's relationship," said Lorna.

Ah, now I know why she is being so secretive. She'll blurt it out one day, she thinks I'm just a dog! Let's wait and see.

Later that day after several breaks and lots of cuddles from some very nice people, we sat down to learn more about angels. Did you know that you can have teams of angels for projects? All you have to do is ask! I love the 'unemployed angels', they are basically angels that you can send to someone who is in need of help. What a great idea, and it keeps them out of mischief!

The day flew by, with lots of chitter chatter and high energy. The humans were all feeling buoyant and ready to face the world with their new found tools and knowledge to help them on this journey of life. We caught the train with less than a minute to spare and as we sat down, number 33 man was a few seats ahead. Mum did a double take and blushed as Lola teased her for her earlier clumsiness. Was this mum opening back up to the possibility of dating? We'll have to wait and see. Mum has so much love to give, yet she often mistakes this for thinking she needs someone to love her to feel complete. If only she could see what she has to offer!

Speedy delivery

As we all arrived home that evening, mum went to the fridge and poured herself and Lola two large glasses of cold crisp Chardonnay, I could smell the notes of apple and wondered what it tasted like. Mum certainly loved it. She spent many a night laughing with

Lola over Chardonnay - if only those bottles could speak, they could definitely tell a story or two. Lola was only popping in for a quick drink as they still hadn't discussed the big news from this morning and the concept for mum's book. Honestly, these two get so distracted, they can talk for hours.

"Louie," she called. What now? I'd just sat down on the sofa but dutifully trotted through to the kitchen and she pointed to my bowl which was sitting in the corner. She had tricked me. The notes of apple had disguised leftover sausages from the fridge that now lay in my bowl looking back up at me. I sat patiently as I've been taught to do, looking at mum lovingly, hanging off her every move, waiting for the go ahead.

"Okay Louie, good boy." she said.

This was my signal to eat. As I tucked into my sausages, sharing them with Bella, I felt gratitude that my earlier order had been fulfilled. I'd completely forgotten about the extra sausages she'd cooked for breakfast. Thank you, mum, angels, Waitrose and whilst we're at it, the whole universe. Now that's how you fulfil your orders.

I could hear mum excitedly filling Lola in on the book and all the ideas. Lola was blown away, she asked lots of questions and mum simply said that she didn't have a clue how she was going to do it, but that she was hopeful that after today, maybe, just maybe, the angels would help and present the right people to her at the right time.

Reflection

A few hours later, Lola and Bella had left for the evening. "What a day!" she said as she flopped into the cuddle chair. I hopped up beside her and cuddled down on her lap. I was waiting for the next unspoken conversation; my coaching shift was not over yet. I knew she would want time to reflect on the day.

"It wasn't too scary for you was it, Louie? The underground was quite busy!"

Scary? It was nothing compared to our day out in Edinburgh when we went to see Marion. Do you not even remember that day out in the city centre?

"Mind you, you have been to Edinburgh and that was quite an adventure."

Yes, exactly. Do you remember when we went to the centre and you insisted on me having my picture taken in as many places as possible? It's a good job I'm a Lord and they let me in.

"Ha ha, the Big Wheel, I can't believe I took you on that."

Me neither, mum. Especially with the pod being made out of glass. That was a test of remaining calm and overcoming a fear of heights. Luckily, because I love you and it wasn't about me that day, it was about you and Marion. I overruled those negative thoughts, put them to one side and got on with enjoying the scenery, even if the castle was in black and white!

"Such great views from the wheel though, the Edinburgh castle looked amazing."

Jeez, does she have to repeat everything, I think? Just as Mum started to laugh, I thought to myself, what now?! Luckily, I won't have to wait long, she tells me everything!

"Louie, do you remember having your photo taken with the reindeer and the bagpiper, he must've been freezing in his tartan kilt?"

Oh yes, I remember that well. The view from the ground, standing by his feet was definitely a different introduction to the young gentleman than you had, mum! It's a good job that I'm not easily offended.

"I wonder if the rumour is true about men in kilts with no undergarments?" said mum.

Well, if only you could hear all my thoughts, then you would know. Next, she'll be talking to me about the whiskey shop.

"What a perfect end to that day in Edinburgh Louie, choosing our whiskey. I can't believe they let you in to do the whiskey tasting!"

A unique bond

So predictable. I think it's time for a nap, I wonder if she'll notice. As my eyes rolled, my beautiful lashes veiled my eyes ready for sleep, and with my head settled into her lap she continued to chatter, only stopping to take a sip of wine. Even reminiscing was different now. She seemed happier and content, as if she was viewing her whole life differently through those rainbow tinted glasses. Maybe I can start retiring from my duties, especially given she has a unique bond with her guardian angel too. I drift in and out of consciousness, catching the odd word here and there.

"When I met my guardian angel, E…, it was the most serene meditation, I'm so pleased I now know her name."

I awoke startled at mum's words. I missed the most important bit, her name! I know she's a 'she' and her name begins with an E. How did I drift off at the most important bit? It's like missing the punch line to a joke. Ah well, there will be plenty more times I'm sure, mum definitely likes to share her thoughts with me. Maybe E doesn't want to be known, after all it is supposed to be a very unique private bond, I won't push this, and I'll just call her, E.

Mum got up, there was one last thing she must do before she finally switched off for the evening. The laptop was out, the printer was on and there it was, a rainbow flowing out of the printer with the title, Be Happy Now - Chasing Rainbows by Lisa

Victoria, the angels and Lord Louie. She let out a sigh of relief as if she was home, right where she needed to be and not just happy in her physical home but also in her heart. In that moment it took pride of place on the vision board.

Well, we best get bonding as a team if we're now off to write a book! Come on E, we can help mum do this!

LORD LOUIE'S LESSONS

1. When was the last time you engaged with other humans and exchanged a smile? Have you stored your 'penguin' jumper away and is it time to get it out?
2. Are you always in so much of a rush that you sometimes become an underground daffodil? What can you do to nurture your growth and see the beauty in life?
3. What are you visualising? Are you focusing on what you have here and now, and what you don't want? Or, are you focusing on what you do have, that you're grateful for, and what you would like in the future?
4. How best would you choose to employ some unemployed angels? They're literally waiting in the wings. Do something good for yourself today and write a list of all the things you want help with. You can include loved ones too if you like. Then simply sit and ask for them to start immediately.
5. Connect with your heart and simply ask your guardian angel to present themselves. Smile at them, ask them what they look like and gently invite them to introduce themselves. What is their name? What message do they have for you today? Just simply listen to what comes into your mind. If at first you can't feel anything, just keep trying.

Discovery — A universal energy

Our angels are close
To light, and guide the way
In moments we feel lost
Just ask, and hear what they say

To the angels, the universe,
Yourself, and much more
Go forth on your journey
Explore what's in store

For life is an adventure
Enjoy this sweet time
Let your heartbeat connect
To the universal chime

This is a new world
Who are they? You say
Universal helpers
To light, and guide the way

Nothing too spiritual
You need no experience
To learn how to access
Their love and their presence

Sometimes a laugh
Sometimes, unconditional love
Always there to be a guide
From way up, up above

In you, they believe
Let them intervene
Your free will and choice
They will not come in-between

The magic they possess
To light and guide your day
Trust in your dreams
Discover a brand-new way

chapter 6

REGRET

'feel sorrow for loss of, wish one could have again.'

Oxford Dictionary

The rise before the fall

M um was on the phone to her friend from university, and they were laughing and chatting. It's the type of friendship where they go for months without speaking and then just pick back up.

"You're kidding me," she says. Uh oh, they are up to something. "Yes, I'm totally up for that, I'd love to support you at your book signing in California. In fact, I'm just looking at my vision board and you'll never guess what, Mike Dooley is in California in May, did you really say January? That's a shame. Maybe my timing is a little out?"

Whaaaat? You're leaving me, I know I love Nana and Gramps but come on, surely you can get me a doggie passport. You said you're staying with Bobbie and Jackson. Aw, come on Mum. If you get to go all the way to America and see your friends, surely, I can come and see my friends too. Bobbie and Jackson are from the same family as me, one is a King Charles Spaniel and the other is a Springer Spaniel. They used to live in the UK but they have embraced the jet set lifestyle and moved to America.

Mum hangs up the phone, after excitedly talking to her friend about California Dreaming. It's wonderful to see her laughing and hopeful about the future.

Love is all around

Bobbie, Jackson and I used to walk lots together. Bobbie and I would meet on the path. I don't think it was always a coincidence, I couldn't contain my excitement when I saw Bobbie and he couldn't either. They were like those film moments, where you haven't seen someone for a while and you drop everything, running towards them in slow motion to embrace, all else is blocked out, your focus is solid. Have you ever experienced that? Well, if you haven't then you should. Don't worry about what others think, it feels amazing! Except we didn't hug, we sniffed each other's ears and danced around excitedly.

I really don't understand why some humans think that you have to find that 'one' special person to feel loved. You are love and love is all around you, if you open your eyes. The great thing about love, is that if you learn to love yourself, without the ego, just pure love for who you are, the magnificence of your being, then you can give more. You can't give something if you haven't created it first, from within, or indeed received it from another source, and by the way, in order to receive something, you've got to be willing to accept. I see so many humans bat off compliments, or if they're offered something, they can't just say thank you. They virtually throw that gift back in the other person's face. Why aren't you good at receiving?

It's an education

Mum is getting there now. Finally! She is still in schooling with me and I believe she will continue to be throughout her life. It's her journey, and so long as she's open to learning she will be in school. She embraces opportunities now to learn, to grow, to be her true authentic self. She's always been good at loving others and supporting them, and now she's finally starting to value herself, learning to receive, feeling deserving of all the good that flows her way and by goodness, once you open that tap, the universe will let it flow.

I've been lost in thought and excitement about how humans can grow, but back to my own predicament. How do I get a passport? Surely, I can find a way to get to America too! Hmmm...

"Aw Louie, as much as I'd love you to come to see Bobbie and Jackson you just can't, it's a long way and it's just not practical for a few weeks, what with quarantine and all. I know you'll have fun with Nana and Gramps."

Humph, I know she's right, so let's focus on what I can have rather than what I can't. Nice long country walks, the log burner, special treatment from the grandparents - don't they just love to spoil us? So yes, that works, I'll choose to be excited about that, rather than sad about mum departing. It will make the reunion all so much more exciting. I'm enjoying running towards her already.

Off I skip into the lounge to get my ball.

"Louie, you are daft. Why are you facing the chair, like some naughty boy scalded in the corner? You do make me laugh, you're so funny."

Ha-ha – but you're not getting it, my ball is trapped, come on, wake up! How can we possibly play ball if you won't do one simple thing for me and help me retrieve my ball. I'm good at lots of things, including coaching you and being your sounding board, but I don't have the long limbs you have to retrieve my ball.

She phones the grandparents to discuss plans for her America trip and craftily sneaks in dog-sitting. Whilst I sit and wait. This isn't working. Let's invoke plan B! If I pace and get her attention then maybe she'll get the hint. If at first you don't succeed, think of a different way. So, I start to pace, I sit in front of her, tilting my head.

"Aw, you should see Louie, mum. He's just staring at me with an adoring look and now he's gone back to the chair and staring under it. He's so funny, what on earth goes through that boy's mind?"

Geez, for humans that have evolved for so many billions of years, sometimes, I really do wonder.

"Oh, you think his ball is stuck… Louie is your ball under there?" She crawls on the floor, phone to one ear and out comes the magical limb as it bends and twists into all sorts of weird positions to reach under the chair. "Ah yes, you were right, his ball was under there."

Honestly, my humans… I'm glad Nana is switched on.

The art of being present

Still on the phone chatting excitedly about her impending trip to America, Mum comes and sits on the floor opposite me in some yoga pose. Legs out straight but apart, creating a V shape. I sit opposite her with my ball and I nudge it with my nose towards her. Sometimes it goes in a straight line but other times it hits her legs. I do try, but I'm not always accurate. Her legs are like the bumpers you get in a bowling alley. If she doesn't create these bumpers with her legs, that's how my ball ends up under the chair. Although, yesterday I created my own fun and decided to play ball on my own, sadly I missed the bumpers so my 'roll it' game came to a grinding halt.

As we sit and play roll it, I am saddened by how distracted she sometimes is, seemingly too busy to just be. I just wish she could be in the moment more often, practicing her to be list rather than ticking off her ever growing to do list. Whilst we're playing ball, she's missing the loving glances I give her, she's not truly with me whilst she's distracted talking on the phone. I don't mind this so much, it's more when you humans scroll mindlessly on social media, sucked into the excitement of what's coming next, or is it just an addiction. I'm so pleased she has downloaded the app to limit how much time she's on her phone, since she's done that, she's definitely more present. I just don't want her to have any regrets later in life.

She's telling Nana all about how she's always wanted to go to California and that she's now starting to say, 'yes' to opportunities. Her new found excitement is real and it's lovely to see.

Full steam ahead

An impromptu evening ensued with Lola and Bella as mum had to share her news about her impending trip to America. As the wine flowed, it became another tipsy night with Lola, they decided to start online dating and had set each other's profiles up, laughing, joking and cringing at the thought of it all, mostly the stigma that was attached to it. I'm not sure what's wrong with meeting online. After all, that's how she found me and goodness knows who else would've kept her on the straight and narrow if I hadn't shown up in her life.

The wine had been flowing which always makes you humans bolder and braver, more daring, often with a few consequences the next day. Questions presenting: Did you really post that on social media last night? Did you really drunkenly phone your ex at 2am to tell him how much you loved him? In addition to nursing a hangover, putting peppermint essential oil on the back of your neck to ease the tension, sitting and dissecting the night before. Where did it all go wrong?

Alcohol can be the green light for relinquishing all your inhibitions. Well, this one night, it had done just that.

Dawning regret

The next morning, we went around to Lola's for coffee and as standard she handed mum the peppermint oil. We sat in the kitchen as Lola cooked a fry up. The smells were divine, the coffee brewing, and a quieter pace compared to the night before.

It was nice to be back at Lola's. It was like a home from home. We were always back and forth between the two houses, but mum has come so far already, I don't think she even notices or has reflected on this. From living with Jim to living with Lola, and now owning her own home, that's quite an achievement and a journey in itself. Do you ever take time to reflect and see how far you have come, or are you always focused on where you feel you need to get to? I hope it's the former.

Lola's phone chimed.

"Who is it?" said mum.

"I don't know, a number I don't recognise." as Lola froze to the spot, clearly something had dawned on her. She started pacing.

"What's wrong, Lola?"

"I think we messaged someone last night, there's a trail of messages and he wants to meet for a dog walk."

"Oh, my goodness," laughed mum. "Are you going to go?"

"Do you think I should?" replied Lola.

"Well why not, if you don't meet people, you'll never find Mr. Right."

"I am not sure, I don't think he is really my type, my gut feeling is saying no, but what if he's okay?"

And therein lies the problem, the gut is saying no, but you're choosing to override it with that nifty piece of kit in your head again. This will be fun to observe. I glance over at Bella and we exchange a knowing look.

"Will you come with me Ellen, just lurk in the background and make sure I'm safe?" asked Lola.

"Of course, we will."

Dating disasters

The following weekend, we were all buckled in the car to drive to a mutual park for a walk. Of course, we had to turn up early so we could separate before Clive arrived. Oh, how Bella and I laughed at the time, as did mum, although I don't think Lola could see the funny side, she was too embarrassed.

Lola put the postcode into the Sat Nav and it instantly said 'make a U turn', well that was the first nudge from the universe. Bella and I looked at each other, this was going to be an entertaining day. Lola hadn't picked up on this sign. Neither had mum. What a pair of bananas they are.

As we were approaching our destination, Lola was trying to figure out where the park actually was and as we turned down the road, we hit a closed road. The Sat Nav chimed, 'make a U turn' and neither of them picked up on the sign again! Eventually we arrived at the gravel car park and mum whisked me out of the car and out of sight. She could've made it a little more inconspicuous, as she hid behind a bush peeking through. I know she was just looking out for Lola but seriously, everyone else walking by from the other side was giving us very strange looks.

A very conservative car pulled into the gravel car park and a very nervous gentleman got out of his car. He had 'Coy Clive' written all over him. Oh goodness, he was not Lola's type at all, acting all coy as he walked over to her.

They walked on ahead of us, mum trying not to make it too obvious. Every time I stopped to water the bushes; she would then feel the need to scurry forwards to catch up on the gap we had lost. Honestly, talk about being subtle.

Teetering on the edge of regret

We caught snippets of the conversation. Coy Clive sounded very desperate as Lola kept walking to the right to create more space between them, body language saying it all. Clive in an attempt to get closer, edged towards Lola to the point she looked like she was tight roping the edge of the path, so as not to fall down the bank into the mud. Bella plodded along; I couldn't wait to hear the entire gossip later on.

By the time we had completed the circuit of the park and we were back in earshot, Clive pretty much declared his undying love for Lola, stating that time was running out and that he would like to take her for dinner to get better acquainted.

"I'm not sure how she is going to wriggle out of this one, Louie." mum chuckled, as I thought the same.

"I'm so pleased she's the one that got the message on the dating app and not me, although I do feel like having a man in my life would be nice, I'm just not sure I am quite ready yet, especially after the whole Jim experience." You will mum, when the time is right. But for now, it's my side of the bed and I'm lapping it up for as long as I can.

As we climbed back into the car mum howled with laughter. "Did you enjoy your date?" she asked. Lola didn't seem to see the funny side. It was a good job they were so close and Lola didn't take offence.

By the time we arrived back at the house and they'd chalked it up to experience, Lola said, "Maybe I should listen to my gut more?"

Yes, maybe you should, and all the signs around you that the universe is constantly presenting! No room for feeling regret though, just a lesson learned.

A farewell meal

The time had come for the America trip. It was the depths of winter and the nights were cold. Lola had invited us around for a farewell, bon voyage meal. Mum had managed to negotiate time off work - the old version of mum wouldn't have even asked for time off at such short notice, worrying about letting her colleagues down, being such a small team and all, succumbing to that feeling of guilt that you humans often practice, especially if you are a sensitive person who puts everyone else before yourself. I'm proud of the changes she's making, slowly, slowly growing into the human being that I can see buried underneath all the doubt and worry. She's finally shedding those layers, unbecoming everything she had been taught to be that didn't serve her, and becoming everything she was born to be.

Luckily, today I didn't have to endure my penguin outfit or my bra in the car, instead we walked. Hooray! More bushes to pee up and my street credibility intact. You see, watering bushes is my profile, the equivalent of your online dating profile, I've got to be out there or how else will I attract my beau. I think we're mainly walking because mum and Lola want a cheeky mid-week, pre-holiday drink. Honestly, any excuse!

Lola had the music playing in the background, nice and low, it's one of my favourite songs, Roar by Katy Perry, and it's very apt for mum's personal development journey. She plays it really loud in the car, I hope she resonates with the lyrics and knows that it was only her own thoughts and beliefs that held her down. Although, I wouldn't recommend 'dancing through the fire'. Dancing, yes, that's great fun. We sometimes do that in the living room but airing on the cautious side, I'd avoid fire unless you're a trained fire walker. Man, are they crazy people?

I'd rather my fire, firmly behind the log burner door, keeping my belly nice and warm.

Lola called through from the kitchen, "Shall I crack open a bottle of wine?"

Was that a rhetorical question? She was asking my mum after all.

As they sat down on the sofa, snuggled up, mum tucked her feet underneath her whilst she cradled her large glass of Merlot, cupped with her hands, staring into it, almost like a crystal ball. She looked really funny from my angle, the glass distorted her face and made her look like she had a huge mouth and a tiny nose, I pawed Bella and she gave me a knowing look. Life can be fun depending on which angle you look at it from.

Past regrets

"Lola, I don't know why I didn't do this sooner, I've been wanting to go away for so long to America, but I kept putting it off, saving money for a rainy day, saving my holidays at work and now finally, I've taken the plunge. I'm super excited. Might as well do it whilst I'm still single. You never know, maybe one day I'll meet my prince."

"Me too, Ellen, we can always hope. And, not a Clive!"

Ooh, maybe mum is teetering on the edge of sharing all that love she has with another human, she does have enough to give.

As they reminisce over their lives, which they often do, they started to question decisions they had made in the past.

"Oh Ellen, I wish I had not immersed myself into my career and focused on having a family. Maybe I would've been happily married now and not divorced. If I could turn the clock back, I would do things differently. I feel like time is running out and that all the decent men are taken."

"I totally hear you," said mum. "When you get to our age, it's almost like living out the life of Bridget Jones. I wish I'd gone travelling when I was younger and not ruled my life with fear of not having enough money, starting my accounting career straight off and moving in with Jim. I wonder how different life would be now?"

I think I may have a nap; this conversation isn't going to exactly create the party vibe ready for holiday.

The first leg of the trip

Saturday came and mum packed the car. The dreaded bra was firmly wrapped around my underarms and shoulders ready for the car journey. I didn't mind it too much, it kept me safe and after all, if I didn't look after mum who would. Although, she seemed to be getting more independent, and would be just fine going to America. Previously, I would have questioned this, but now, with her new found hope and tool kit, I'm confident she'll survive at least. Maybe, even thrive.

"Come on Louie, hop in," mum said, as she clunk clicked my seat belt in. I will miss her, but I'm excited for her too. This is what I don't understand about you humans, you have been programmed to find the bad. With mum going away, even Lola said the other night, "it's going to be terrible, what will I do without you? I'll miss you".

Why couldn't she see it as an opportunity to gather more stories and excitement for when they catch up, and be happy for mum rather than thinking about 'poor me', what am I going to do whilst you're gone? That's coming from a place of lacking and Lola will spend the time feeling low, thinking about what fun she's missing out on, the dreaded FOMO, fear of missing out. Goodness me! I'm not going to have FOMO, I'm going to smile at the thought of mum having fun and be pleased for her, not jealous or aggrieved because she didn't get me a doggie passport.

I'm choosing to enjoy my pampering at Nana and Gramp's. I'm not going to sit and wallow, and waste my precious time waiting. I'm going to create fun.

Shoulda, coulda, woulda

Mum put the postcode for Wales into the Sat Nav. Even though she knows the way, she likes to check for traffic and today we had a diversion. She tuts as it states that there is a road closure. "Blooming heck," she says, "typical, we should've left earlier, then we would have avoided this road closure." Oh, here we go again, regret creeping in. See it does this, oh so subtly. Maybe we would've missed the road closure, but maybe we wouldn't, there's no point in wasting energy on it now, it's happened. Come on mum, I'm cheering from the back of the car, just choose, you can't change it.

"Ah well, Louie, we'll just have to put some music on, sing and have fun, it will take as long as it takes." Wow! That was quick choosing for mum, normally she mumbles and curses about how it's not fair and that it always happens to her for most of the journey, winding herself up and getting more frustrated, beeping at cars. Goodness knows, sometimes even speeding just to shave a minute off the time and arriving all in a fluster and exhausted… but Bingo, she's definitely developing. Yippee! My heart was swelling with pride. All my efforts weren't in vain.

As we drive, mum turns the music down. "Do you know…" she says, oh dear here we go again, it's one of those conversations she has with herself, but pretends she's talking to me to convince herself she's not going mad. "I love the Sat Nav concept of life, Louie. We put so much trust in the Sat Nav to get us to Nana and Gramp's house three hours away, we pop in the destination and we don't even question the route, or where we are, an hour in, or indeed panic or feel hopeless because we think we're lost and we won't arrive. We just trust, merrily. I wish I had realised that sooner, life wouldn't have been so hard."

Yes mum, you're absolutely right, it's about enjoying the journey and not hankering for the destination. Sing along to the radio, and enjoy the scenery! I love these conversations with her, she's definitely blossoming.

Regret free weekend

We had a wonderful weekend catching up with Nana and Gramps with lots of trips to the beach where I like to take a dip in the water and run in and out of the sand dunes. It's a great place to play tip and hide. Mum loves this because she gets to take my picture, camouflaged into the background so she can play, 'Where's Lord Louie' on Facebook with her friends. When we're in Wales, mum almost melts the minute we get there, the fresh sea breeze and brisk walks, and my goodness can they be brisk. Stresses are forgotten momentarily until she loses her real self again, lost under the overwhelm of life and the constant to do list. Although recently, she is more in the moment, and not just in Wales.

"So, love, have a super time in America, we will look after your dog." says Nana as mum climbed into the car. Dog? Nana, that's not quite right. I look up at her adoringly, held safely in her arms, I nudge her face gently to show my disapproval. "Sorry Lord Louie, how did the D word slip out of my mouth?" That's OK Nana, I forgive you, Lord it is.

A winter retreat

Later that evening, mum called to say she'd arrived home, excited for her upcoming trip when the news broke. There had been an ash cloud and all travel was suspended at least for a few days. Oh dear, I wonder how mum will cope with this. Ha, well isn't this ironic, normally she jet sets and leaves me home, but how the tables have turned. I'm now on my retreat in Wales and she's grounded in England.

The next day, I skipped down the stairs, past my angel sign and thanked them for my wonderful retreat. Mum couldn't go on holiday, but I certainly was enjoying myself. As Nana came down the stairs after me, she opened the front door. I stood, staring in disbelief, the farm was white all over, not a bit of green in sight. I leapt out the front door trying to remember where all my favourite bushes were for me to water, the snowfall was disguising all sorts of smells. I loved the snow. My retreat was getting better by the day.

As I leapt back in the house, Nana was at the ready with a treat for me. I've got her well trained. She just can't resist my head tilts. I ran upstairs to wake Gramps up, excited for the day ahead. My winter retreat is really coming together now.

"Aw Louie, not yet, I'm reading my paper." said Gramps. Oh, come on, how often does it snow? You can read your paper later. It suddenly dawned on me, even though I thought I was off duty, I'm now coaching Gramps and probably Nana too. Ah well, at least I've got my qualifications for this role, mum is a tough client. I think my years of experience will come in handy.

It took an hour of pacing for Nana and Gramps to finally give in. They put on their wellie boots and off we started, up the mountain. Nana and Grampa were throwing snowballs at each other and laughing and having fun. I saw them truly light up. I love the saying, 'we don't stop playing games because we grow old; we grow old because we stop playing games', by George Bernard Shaw. One thing I couldn't quite fathom was where the snowball went. I know sometimes when we play 'roll it' with my tennis ball it gets lost under the chair, but where do the snowballs go when they land. I've searched high and low for them, dug for them, but it's a mystery.

"Louie, you just don't understand," said Gramps as he smiled and laughed. You're right, I don't, please don't mock me. Humph. We spent hours outside playing, Gramps even built a snowman. I can't wait to tell mum how much fun we've had.

As we arrived back at the farmhouse, it was cosy and warm. I stood in the outhouse whilst Nana tried to get the snowballs off my feet. That's the thing with being a long-haired spaniel, the snow goes into balls and sticks all the way up my legs. It's a good job I can laugh at myself and I don't mind them laughing at me, happy in my own skin with who I am, not worrying about my image.

I stood helpless until Gramps had a great idea, a bowl of warm water. Oooh goodie, a foot spa too. This is better than humans describe their ski holidays. I get to play in the snow, have a foot spa, and sit by the log burner to toast my feet. The only thing that would put the icing on the cake would be the equivalent of a nice glass of something après-ski style.

Once my toes had been dried next to the wood burner in the lounge, I was starting to feel sleepy. Nana called me through. "Come on Louie, time for dinner." As I trotted through to the kitchen, well, my oh my, thoughts do become things. Nana had dished up my dinner. "As a treat tonight, Louie, you can share our dinner. Sausages and broccoli." Wowsers, my own sausage dinner. "And because it's a fun day, let's celebrate! I've made a Prosecco for me and Gramps and a Pawsecco for you." Oh, my goodness, après-ski indeed. I'm living the dream. Are you? If not, why not? It's never too late, and you are never too old to make changes.

Doom and gloom

The news seemed to unfold, like some sort of a dream. Every day that Gramps turned the television on, the world was going mad. There was a Global Pandemic in the making and people were being warned not to travel. Chaos was ensuing. Surely this wasn't all real?

An hour or so later, the mobile started ringing. I hope that's mum so I can tell her about my day. It was, and I could see her on WhatsApp. Yay!

"So, what's happening with your flight, will you get your money back?" Gramps said.

"No, it's being postponed until we come out of lockdown. Can you believe this whirlwind, so much can change in so little time? I was so looking forward to going away. I've always put my dreams on hold, never had the confidence to just say yes, and now look. I'm full of regret. I should've done this sooner. What if I never get to go? And to top it off, the borders have been closed so, even if I wanted to come to Wales to get Louie, I can't and I'm snowed out, it's a total disaster."

Wow! She seemed all doom and gloom today. Poor mum, she's worked so hard on her resilience, self-love and belief in the universe, angels and higher energy. I hope she doesn't regress now.

A postcard from Wales

In a last-ditch attempt to cheer mum up, even if I was 200 miles away at the other end of a phone call, I ran through to the kitchen and back again, Nana looking perplexed until she realised, I wanted her to follow me. It's like a game of charades with humans. You eventually get it, but sometimes it takes a little effort.

I sat by my bowl of Pawsecco and Nana said, "Oh, you want some more Pawsecco?" We're getting closer. I want you to tell mum about our day so she wakes up and stops feeling sorry for herself. Something like this...

"Dear Mum, I'm having a whale of a time at my country's winter retreat. Usually, you go off on holiday and leave me at home, but this time, I'm off on my winter holidays instead!

It's rather nice here, I get to play catch the snowball but I can't find them when they land, I've no idea where they go.

In the afternoon, the grandparents make me a warm foot bath to get rid of my snowball feet before I retreat to an armchair by the log burner after a yummy dinner and a glass of Pawsecco.

Sorry you missed your winter trip this year, but I'm making up for it, for you.

Yours,
Lord Louie"

"Shall I tell you about our day and what we've been up to?" said Nana to Mum, over the phone.

Yes, finally. I sometimes wonder if humans are subconsciously telepathic. You do get there eventually.

Distant longing

Mum seemed quite disinterested, she was stuck on the negative loop of frustration and regret. She couldn't see past it, the joy of our day, she was trapped in the 'poor me' record.

"I've been speaking to Lola on Zoom and we're both totally fed up. I can't believe I didn't do these things sooner. I should've gone last year, then I would've had Louie with me for lockdown, instead I have four walls and I feel quite lonely and isolated." Mum said to Nana. You could hear the tears in her voice. A gentle soul, now feeling lost.

Nana looked at me again. I best put my coaching hat back on. As Nana tilted the camera towards me, I felt like a performing monkey. I know I'm good but jeez, how to handle this one. So, I started doing my Yoga, mum always thinks it's cute, I do my down dog first and then my up dog followed by shoulder surfing, a play bow and then yap excitedly. This usually makes her smile, putting the fun back in.

But today, nothing.

Weathering the storm

"I can't even come to Wales to see you and Louie," said mum. Well, sometimes you just have to batten down the hatches and weather the storm. It's okay to feel like this, she'll get through it. I know, because humans always do, you're way more resilient than you know. This isn't the worst storm she's weathered either, I've heard all the stories she's told Lola. It's okay to not be okay, just like the cloudy days, the sun is still always shining. You just can't always see it. I'm off for another drink of Pawsecco, it's the only solution.

Nana continued the conversation as I left the room, "Come on love, all this personal development you've been telling us about, this is the time to dig deep and use it."

We were losing mum. Such a sensitive soul, the wind had been taken out of her sails. It was like she was relapsing, back to the time when her brake line went on the motorway.

"What's the point in all this vision board stuff? I feel silly for even trying to think it would work. So much time has been wasted trying to be positive, visualising my future and it's all being met with roadblocks, just when something good is about to happen. The book signing event is now on zoom and all I wanted to do was go to California. I finally had the confidence to say yes and now the only places I have to go are the supermarkets in Towcester."

At least you get to go to the book signing, mum. Remember you've still got your L plates. You've not perfected this yet, but you will.

Black magic

Several weeks passed and nothing had changed. We were still in lockdown. Apart from one big change that was happening in mum's life.

She called in floods of tears, she sounded distraught. The events had unfolded with her work and her accounting practice could no longer weather the storm. They were already struggling and they had been offered a deal by an American company. It was redundancy or relocation. Oh dear, maybe one day she'll pass her test in the Law of Attraction. She really didn't think it through when she created her vision board with her 'L' plates.

Mum, feeling low in self-confidence and not being able to see the wood for the trees, opted for relocation, fearful of not having a job. Ed, her boss, had been really supportive, yet she was struggling. The idea of relocating seemed attractive at the time but when it came to it, fear crept in and the reality of not seeing family as often, as well as all the other practicalities, mum was torn and feeling out of control.

She bared her heart and soul. Worrying about how she was going to relocate us, and get me a passport (finally), regretting buying a house and having the financial commitment. Would she sell her house? Rent it out? She'd hit rock bottom and boy; did she feel it. Feeling overwhelmed by the future, rather than excited for the next adventure. She was filled with so much uncertainty and the one thing she was losing was belief, trust in the universe and the angels. If there was ever a time to ask for help, it was now.

I rooted for her. Knowing that when you hit rock bottom, there is only one way to go! Sadly, she couldn't see this. She was deep in regret. Regret of what she should have, could have, and would have done differently if she were to have her time again. She was looking back, not being present and not trusting in the future. Yet, the last time she spiralled into an abyss that fateful day on the motorway, the angels and universe were there to catch her when she fell, spring boarding her back on to her rightful path. Sometimes they just simply have to intervene.

LORD LOUIE'S LESSONS

1. Are you good at receiving compliments? If not, think about how you will respond positively next time to someone giving you a compliment.
2. Are you present as often as you should be? Is there anything you can change to be more present with loved ones in your life to prevent later regrets?
3. Do you sometimes get gut feelings but ignore them? What will you do next time you have a decision to make?
4. Are you truly being the person you were born to be? If not, shall we start today?
5. Do you embrace the journey, or are you missing the moment whilst racing towards the destination?
6. Do you sometimes lose faith? Just take a moment to reflect on times in your life that you have survived and come out stronger. You've got this. Just have faith, belief in yourself, and most importantly practice self-love.

Regret

Regret is a feeling
That no longer serves
One of pain and sorrow
Thoughts all a fuzz

We coulda, shoulda, woulda
Done things differently before
Negative thoughts crying out
Wanting more, more, more

For when we feel regret
We lose sight of gratitude
It affects our outlook
And indeed, our attitude

Hindsight is wonderful
And should be used wisely
Life's not lacking
Burdened or miserly

Hindsight is the foresight
Lessons we have learned
Used for the future
To create a life what's yearned

Think not of regret
No room for self-pity
For the future is within you
Feel hope and opportunity

Turn your regrets into lessons
A signpost for what's next
No longer procrastinating
Or feeling all perplexed

Regret is a gift
To fuel hopes and dreams
A life you deserve
Contentment bursting at the seams

chapter 7

BREAKTHROUGH

"an important discovery or event that helps to improve
a situation or provide an answer to a problem"

Cambridge Dictionary

An epiphany

Several days had passed. I had hoped mum was okay. Sometimes humans just need some space to reflect. As the phone rang and Nana answered it, it was mum.

The pesky vision board she blurted down the phone. Her voice seemed to have a laughing lilt to it. I'm not sure if she was laughing or crying.

She went on to explain how she had sat down to reflect on what to do next, with the uncertainty in her life around her impending relocation, when her vision board fell off the wall and came crashing down onto the floor. Papers that she had pinned on, some of them became loose and were floating down through the air. The last one to land was 'redundancy or relocation'.

She described that moment as surreal. Her faith restored in the angels and the universe. Not only had they woken her up with the crashing of the board onto the floor to get her attention - it was the neighbour drilling a hole next door which caused the vibration - they had pointed out to her loud and clear that her wish had been heard and it had been granted.

She was back to her true self. Luckily, mum has had a breakthrough. Hoorah!

As she was talking to Nana she said, "Hey! Do you remember me saying, you can't change the situation but you can choose how you respond to it? Well, I had momentarily forgotten that everything is a choice. I was paralysed in fear. I have decided to embrace the move and if for whatever reason it doesn't work out, there are always options."

Wow, I'm one proud owner of my human. When times are tough, it's how we perceive the situation. Life happens all the time. Through the ups and downs humans always learn, you find your resilience and you grow stronger. It's not about waiting for the external to be 'fixed', it's about changing the internal perception. True change comes from connecting with your true self, and choosing your response.

There is a great quote by Charles R. Swindoll, 'Life is 10% what happens to you and 90% how you react'. Now there's one from under my collar.

Angelic whispers

Not long after her vision board had landed on the floor, mum had decided to do a meditation to connect with her guardian angel. She discovered that her significance of life was to 'be' in the moment, trust, and let life catch up. She was exactly where she needed to be right now and indeed where she had asked to be. I do hope she's updated her vision board now with her next destination.

Her guardian angel, E, guided her to realise that she didn't need any more to be happy. No more money, time, love, qualifications, friends, or acceptance. All she had to do was to practice being grateful for what she had. Opportunities abound. This was a big one. Opportunity versus adversity. Which one would you choose?

E showed her how to feel grateful and that there are always options. She could sell her house, rent her house, pivot and change direction, goodness forbids, embrace life and opportunity, and live.

E taught mum to believe and trust. It's all about perspective. When you work from a place of gratitude it changes everything, like attracts like, lack attracts lack. Wanting more attracts wanting more, abundance attracts abundance. It's the law. The Law of Attraction!

Yes! I wag my tail excitedly - she's finally got it, thank you E and the universe for waking mum up, holding her hand and guiding her. Can we have a party to celebrate please? Wait! We best wait for the lockdown to be over. Now that's going to be one 'Ellen' of a party. See what I did there? Go on laugh, you know you want to!

Surviving to thriving

E has seemingly been guiding her more since I've been in Wales. We're almost like a relay team. I get the feeling I'm going to be carrying the baton again soon, but I'm excited by this. You're never alone, there is always a team around you. Family, friends, angels, earth angels in disguise as animals. If she survived the period of her life where multiple things were happening at once, what is so worrying about now? You may think that you can't do it this time, but even published authors who write books sometimes have the chatter that says they can't write a book. What an absolute lie, they're a published author so where is the evidence? If they can do it once, why can't they do it again?

E has shown mum that the time in her life, that she thought everything was crumbling around her, is actual proof that she's more resilient than she thinks, and indeed more like Morph than she knows (more on Morph later). As if she heard my thoughts, as she always does...

"Well, I was thinking," mum went on to explain to Nana. "If I survived that, why wouldn't I survive what the world is going through now? There is light at the end of the tunnel, if we choose to think this and have faith, knowing that we will be taken care of and the right things will happen at the right time to get us back on the path to our true being. I mean, that sequence of events led me to a Reiki session, which was most relaxing. It's as if the world was telling me to slow down."

Ironic too, given your brake-line went, you were actually speeding up before you came to a grinding halt! Thank goodness there wasn't a policeman nearby.

Huge insights from mum.

You humans are amazing at surviving and its now time to start thriving. Keep your thoughts positive, remain in hope and look for the good in each situation. What can you possibly be grateful for today? Even the small stuff, waking up in the morning, maybe that's the really big stuff! Everything else can be created again if you give yourself permission to be hopeful. For when you ask your brain these questions, it can't help but look for answers.

Destination happiness

"What are you planning on doing for the rest of the week?" asked Nana.

Mum went on to explain that she was taking time to really dream big about her future, no longer held back in limiting beliefs or worrying about what people would think. She discovered this when she was connecting with E.

She was going to sit down and update her vision board, really connecting with her heart's desires, and this time she was going to be careful what she wished for. Focusing on what feelings she wanted - a creative fulfilling career, health and happiness, and fun. She was still going to leave some of the things on there like the red convertible, because why not. If you don't think about it, it won't be. After all, she works hard and deserves some reward.

Time is a gift. It's there for you to reflect, re-set and get ready for the future. It's nice to have something to look forward to, to inspire you and a reason to get out of bed in the morning.

Living not lolling

Mum was on a roll. She told us how she had set up some zoom meetings with Lola and they were going to have a 'virtual' party. She was becoming the change. Or in the words of Mahatma Gandhi, 'Be the change you wish to see in the world' and mum was certainly starting to change from the inside out.

Mum went on to explain that she was done with 'lolling' and wanted to start living.

Nana and Gramps started telling her, when they were at school, they were taught not to get too excited in case they ended up disappointed.

Well blow me down. Is that what you humans are taught? Not to get excited, just in case it actually goes well? Well, that goes against the Law of Attraction and also steals away the joy of the moment. Remember, we talked about the children in our extended family and how they behave at Christmas? Have you ever seen them sit there with a present in their lap saying 'I daren't get too excited before I open this present because it might be something I don't want'? Or, are they animated with energy as they rip the paper expectantly, then shout, 'yes, this is what I've always wanted'? Nine times out of ten they get what they want, but if they don't, they pick themselves back up, dust themselves off and look around to see the pile of presents and then focus on the ones they like. They seldom sit, staring at the one they don't like, focusing all their energy there. They move on, displaying resilience, shifting their focus and energy. Then you humans spoil it and become adults, losing this sparkle, lolling along instead of living. Can you relate? Stop adulting so much and release your inner child more.

Earth angel observations

From my observation of humans, your biggest breakthroughs come from your moments when you are experiencing feelings of being lost or low. These are the times for opportunity and significant growth. Without these moments, you wouldn't be able to appreciate the better times.

I love that wherever you go, life is an adventure. You never know just who you are going to meet or the magical impact that a chance meeting or introduction could have on your life. This happens to humans all the time. It just takes one minute, one hour, one day, one phone call, or one flat tyre at the side of the road for the universe to magically create a situation that helps you along your journey. Are you looking for these signposts? Are you seeing them or hearing them and then taking action?

I remember not so long ago, every time we got in the car, the same song would always come on the radio. It was Hold on Tight, by Electric Light Orchestra. Mum used to tut and get frustrated, muttering that she was sick of it. I sat quietly in the back as I always do, chuckling to myself. She was missing the gentle nudge from the universe, the words in the song were so apt. It was at a time in our lives that she felt lost, way before her personal development had really started and she was feeling down beat about life.

Opportunity knocks

Later that week, mum called on zoom, excited to chat through her news.

"Hi Ellen, how are you?" asked Nana and Gramps.

"You'll never guess what's happened?" said mum.

She had my attention. What on Earth has she been up to in my absence? I hope no more online dating with Lola.

"Do you remember how I've always wanted to share hope with the world after that life changing moment with the motorway and the brake-line?"

My human grandparents nodded in complete understanding.

"Well, yesterday when I was talking with Lola, she mentioned that she'd been speaking with her cousin who is the podcast producer and that he's looking for someone to share some stories of hope. I never even knew that her cousin John did podcasting. After all these years! Funny how timing is always so pertinent! Just today, I had a zoom call with him and we recorded a podcast on positivity in the face of adversity."

I could hear the excitement in her voice.

"That's amazing," said Nana, "How did you feel about that?"

"Well, of course I was scared thinking about speaking to thousands of people around the world, but I chose to step outside of my comfort zone and just do it. And, I absolutely loved it! This is the feeling that we can have when we step outside of our comfort zones. I had so much fun, nothing bad happened and I'm so grateful I said yes and followed my gut."

Ah, that gut feeling. It's never wrong. Another Sat Nav, gently steering you in life, cheering you on and encouraging you.

"Wasn't that on your vision board, Ellen?" asked Nana. Ooh, well remembered Nana. The picture of the microphone!

"Yes, it was! After all this time, I didn't even need to leave the house! Funny how things come to fruition when we just let them be."

I am really starting to feel redundant here with my coaching skills. I wonder if she is going to ask to see me!

"Where's Louie?" Oh goodness, that was a quick 'thoughts becoming things'. I really must be careful what I think.

"Louie!" called Nana, come and hear mum's news.

I sat like a good boy staring at the screen, mum all animated. Shining!

"Are you having fun at Nana and Gramps?"

Is she silly, us four legged friends are seldom not in the moment?

"So, what's on for the rest of the week, Ellen?" asked Gramps.

"Planning our move to America, I need to get the relocation paperwork done and sort out Louie's travel documents."

It's real. We're actually going to America to relocate. A passport finally. I hope Nana and Gramps will come to visit.

"So, you're actually going? Do you have a date yet? Ironic, given you wanted to visit and now you're moving there." said Gramps.

"No firm dates yet, but it will likely be in the next few months before summer."

"Ooh, a feather has just appeared in front of me, how delightful, gotta fly." and that was mum off the phone. I'm so pleased she saw the feather; she is noticing signs now. Feathers mean that angels are nearby. I wonder what they are telling her now.

Just as mum was leaving the zoom call, I could hear Alexa in the background. I could swear she was playing the only way is up, by Yazz!

Breakthroughs

I'm so pleased mum had this major breakthrough. Sometimes, it takes time and it's a journey. I get humans are complex beings and it really doesn't always serve you having that clever piece of kit in your head. Whilst it does help in many ways, it also hinders in others, especially based on the programming you have wired in throughout life, often through no fault of your own. Please, if nothing else, don't spend too much time in your head. So much more fun happens when you're guided by your heart voice and your gut.

Experience life. Push yourself out of your comfort zone and into the magic zone. Enjoy the phenomenal experiences and if it doesn't go to plan, what lesson did you learn and remember to morph yourself back to the real you who is happy, centred and ready to move on experiencing life.

LORD LOUIE'S LESSONS

1. If the event is only 10%, how can you possibly change your response to situations you have going on in your life right now?
2. Are you living in fear or are you living in the excitement of abundance? How can you shift this?
3. What have you survived in the past that's bigger than what you're experiencing now?
4. What lies have you been listening to in your head about what you can't do?
5. Please give yourself some time to reflect and truly listen to what will make you get out of bed in the morning. Big or small. A hobby or a job, just something!
6. How can you spend more time in your magic zone living, as opposed to your comfort zone lolling?

Breakthrough

When you feel like life is tough
Spiralling all the way down
Take a step away
Don't fret, fear or frown

Take this time to reflect
For in this moment, you will see
You're falling to the bottom
To bounce back and be free

Moments of realisation
How much you have grown
Lessons learnt along the way
Otherwise, wouldn't be known

Connect with your heart
Tune into your gut
Drown out the cries
The unhelpful 'yeah but'

For you can achieve
Your heart's desire
When you learn how
Your brain to rewire

Change your I can't
Into I can
The unhelpful opinion
You're no longer a fan

Shorten the pathways
That no longer serve
Practice the new ones
You know you deserve

You are a magical being
Just believe in you
Take a step today
And see what you breakthrough

chapter 8

THE JOURNEY

''an act of travelling from one place to another,
especially when they are far apart'

Oxford English Dictionary

Bouncebackability

I f only humans knew how much you are like 'Morph'. For those of you who watched TV in the 80s, there was an animated plasticine character called Morph. He would bend and flex into any shape but would always return to his smiley, happy self. I wasn't around then, but mum has watched it on YouTube. It's quite entertaining if you want a bit of light fun.

Some people call it bouncebackability, others call it the Tigger Syndrome. Whatever you want to call it, do you have that protection on your life? Most people don't. Mum didn't, but now she has some anti-virus software for her thoughts and some faith in trusting things will turn out just fine. When faced with adversity, she used to take it personally. Every slight negative comment, rejection, or change in external circumstances, was because something was wrong with her. People would say, toughen up, and when you're sensitive, that's just not helpful.

But now she knows, she's ready to pass the 'L' plates on to someone else. Becoming the driving instructor to guide them on their journey. She has now officially bounced back.

Over the next few weeks, the podcast was released. She'd met this event with both worry and excitement. Worry about what others thought, but also excited that she had enjoyed sharing her journey so much. Her true light was shining. Mum went on to explain that as soon as she had listened to the podcast, it reminded her to start focusing her energy on what possibilities the relocation could present to her. You all need reminding from time to time! Soon after the release of the podcast, she had a welcome meeting with her new boss in America. Ed her current boss had excitedly, like a proud work dad, told them all about the podcast. Mum reacted with embarrassment, but then quickly turned this into pride. Swift work mum! You're getting the hang of this now. Her new boss asked mum if she would be open to a slight role change. They wanted her, as part of her job, to coach the newly forming team through transformation, using her skills as a professional, but also the tools she had embraced on her personal journey.

Well, you can just imagine mum's reaction, she was on cloud nine. Creating her future and now steering the ship with her team around her.

Here she is again being invited back into flow. Sharing her experiences to give hope to people during uncertain times and times of change. Another thing that was on her vision board. It's magical how these wishes come to fruition, she'd still be doing the accounting job yet she's going to be getting fulfilment from this on another level by adding in the coaching. She couldn't have planned this any better had she tried. Sometimes you just have to trust, say yes to opportunities, and find the gifts in disguise along your journey. Remember happiness is not a destination.

Reunited on our journey

It was early May and as we started to ease out of lockdown, mum arrived in Wales. It was time for the next leg of our journey. America, here we come! The daffodils had tailed off and we were coming into summer. She looked different, not just physically, but energetically. Her hair was longer. Her skin was radiant. She looked healthier and happier apart from her roots and grey hairs, but please don't tell her I said that. My hair was long too, I was starting to look more like a Shetland pony than a Cocker Spaniel. Last time mum tried to home clip me, she took a chunk of hair out of my bottom as I wriggled in fear before she admitted defeat and I ran for cover.

Hopefully, we can both have a trip to the groomers now this whole lockdown is lifted. I know she likes having her eyebrows and nails done too. I personally think she's naturally beautiful but there's no harm in having these things done because you want to, not just because you need to in order to feel prettier.

The reunion was just as I had dreamed. Like meeting my friend Bobbie on the path. Yet, this time it was mum running towards me, our eyes locked, unconditional love spoken right there in a look. She scooped me up in her arms as I cried with excitement, tears of joy rolling down mum's cheeks. The realisation for mum that what truly matters isn't the big house, car, or fancy clothes, it's having someone to embrace.

Mum and Nana embraced each other and stood for at least 20 seconds before Mum hugged Gramps for 20 seconds.

Did you know, hugging someone you love for 20 seconds a day is the key to alleviating stress and beating burnout? A lingering embrace releases the bonding hormone oxytocin, which can lower your blood pressure, slow your heart rate and improve your mood. Who doesn't like a hug?! Now you know! Sometimes, I even surprise myself with these nuggets of wisdom.

As mum settled on the sofa, I jumped up on her lap. I placed one paw on her leg so she couldn't escape and I placed my head in her lap as she cuddled me. It's the little moments that make memories and this was one of them.

This was it. This was the beginning of our American journey. Mum had packed her suitcase to leave and everything else was in transit. I wasn't going back to Towcester for now, I was California bound. The wonderful grandparents took us to the airport. The last few months had seen mum planning, and it was finally happening.

Memory lane

The following day was so magical, making more memories. We went to the beach and as I ran in and out of the sand dunes, mum embraced her inner child playing tip chase with me. It was such a fun game. I'm so pleased she hasn't gotten old and stopped playing. I hid amongst the grass in the dunes and when she found me, I'd run off just as she was just about to catch me. We paddled on the beach in the little pools of water. The sun was starting to get some heat now we were approaching summer, and there were seagulls flying overhead, chirping as they do.

Walking along, we heard the music of an ice cream van. Now, I know Nana and Gramps would have had one and even shared it with me, but mum was an advocate of healthy living and that sugar is bad for us so maybe we wouldn't get to share our secret today.

"Let's get an ice cream?" mum said. She proceeded to get three ice creams and as they posed for a selfie, grey roots and all, they smiled, ice cream around their mouths, beaming from ear to ear. Without a second thought, mum uploaded the photo to Facebook. Wow! What a transformation from the wellington boots photo. She clearly no longer was worrying what others would think.

We sat and the view was stunning, we were all in the moment which was truly spectacular because it is so unusual to have so many humans collectively being, all at the same time. The energy was peaceful, the gentle breeze brushed past my fur. The seagulls were threatening to steal our precious ice cream as they swooped and dived, but luckily Gramps was on hand to shoo them away and nothing phased anyone. It was as if a new calm, serene peace had descended over everyone. Maybe our guardian angels were joining us for an ice cream.

Laughter from children flowed, carried by the breeze. Other dogs were playing ball and colourful kites were flying. It was wonderful to see and experience this new way of living. People seemed to appreciate each other more. It's almost as if they were practicing gratitude, being thankful for what they had, slowing down from a pace of rush, rush, rush, to appreciating the beauty around them in every moment. It was even more wonderful that mum had slowed down and I could see that she was taking all of this in too. No longer lost in future planning or projecting, and still, in the moment to witness the beauty of life. How often are you still in the moment? Do you really see life around you come alive?

"So, what time is Lola coming tomorrow?" asked Nana.

"First thing in the morning!"

Whaaaaaat? Is Bella coming too? They were all so focused on the peacefulness of the beach, nobody answered my question. I pawed them, sat in front of them with head tilts, and they just thought that I wanted to play. Maybe I needed to sharpen my communication skills a little. I think I've been in holiday mode for too long.

Masterful morning

The next morning, mum woke up early. In fact, before me. This is a far cry from when we used to come to Wales and I had to encourage her to get out of bed.

"Come on Louie. We've got a new morning routine to do.".
Excellent, she's discovered her own masterful morning in my absence.

She ran downstairs, energised and happy to be up. She passed the angel sign on the stairs and said, 'thank you guardian angel for being by my side and gifting me another beautiful morning'.

I ran with her. Excited at this new found energy for mornings, also thanking the angels. I'm actually starting to see my real mum more of the time. She's definitely been continuing on her journey whilst I've been at my winter retreat. How do you start your morning? Accidentally or deliberately? Mum definitely used to be accidental in her approach. I'm enjoying her new structure which sets her up for the day.

Given that it was a nice sunny morning, we retreated to the garden. The pink and yellow miniature dahlias were in full bloom, as were the orange and yellow marigolds. She had picked a perfect spot to place down her glass of water, skipped back into the house all excited and a moment later, came out with her yoga mat, vision board, journal and some affirmation cards.

She flicked her yoga mat out across the grass and as it floated down onto the lawn, it settled into place. It had a beautiful print of a dead dandelion on it. Don't worry, the dead dandelion is beautiful. Many humans pick them and make a wish. They're called 'pappus' in this state. Mum has picked a good mat here. When was the last time you picked a pappus, embracing the inner child and made a wish?

Meditative moment

Mum put on a guided meditation and positioned herself on the mat in savasana. I lay at her feet, observing the process. The meditation played on mum's phone. She started with slow mindful breaths and then it went deeper into a guided meditation where you were instructed to focus on pure relaxation.

As the meditation finished, mum slowly sat up, looking relaxed. It had only been ten minutes yet; I could see the huge impact it had on her. Did you know that meditation can upregulate your immune system if you practice it consistently? It's to do with the brainwaves. Have you ever experienced guided meditation? I promise you, it's not completely whacky, it's very relaxing and I invite you to try it.

Create today's journey

Next, she reached for her pretty journal, it was like a magical energy was coming off it. She couldn't wait to open it and start writing. With the pen in her left hand, the words were unfolding across the page, tumbling out her thoughts and feelings, ordering them into place for the day ahead.

She momentarily glanced back and forth at her vision board. There have been a few updates since I last saw it.

She sat looking at her vision board, really focused and I could see her not just thinking about it, but really feeling what it's like to be living that life. Her stare piercing the board and then looking up into the blue sky, wishing, pondering and really getting into that feeling, like stepping into the world of Narnia but without physically moving and using the invisible pappus to blow her wishes out into the universe.

Do you journal your thoughts and create your day intentionally? Or, do you roll out of bed and hit the ground running, the day taking over you?

Dreams and intentions

As part of the next exercise in her masterful morning, she shuffled her affirmation cards and simply asked, 'what do I need to focus on today'. Moments later she selected a card from the pack and read the words aloud.

"Dare to dream, whatever your heart desires, it's closer than you think and more achievable than you can imagine." She breathed a sigh of acceptance and once more picked up her journal and started writing, firstly recording the affirmation for the day and then what this meant to her. Dreams and expectations flowing across the page with no doubt creeping in to worry about the how, they were just pure, raw dreams from within her heart.

It was such a proud moment for me. Such a shift in mum, deliberately starting her day with intention and no longer playing small. Her dreams were important and she was now open to reaching for them, she had a newfound inner confidence in her being.

What intentions do you set in the morning?

Do you value your dreams enough to even believe them possible? Just try it. I dare you!

Morning movement

Now came a spot of yoga. Mum now realised how important exercise was as part of a morning routine, I liked that she had chosen yoga, something I am also good at. Nana arrived just in time to be roped in too.

This is the easy bit for me, down dog and up dog, I'm just a natural. We all lined up as mum gave instructions to Nana on what to do and I demonstrated to help. Nana laughed as she collapsed from up dog. I walked over to sniff her ears, I knew this would tickle and she cried, "Louie stop!" half with laughter, her arms tucked under her.

I love seeing humans laugh, you can't possibly be unhappy and laugh at the same time. Now there's a simple way to be happy. Laugh more. Don't quote me on the facts but it's something like children laugh ten times as often as adults. That means if an adult laughs 20 times a day, then children are having 200 laughs. I'm pleased I'm not a human but if I was, then I definitely would reconnect with my inner child as I grow up and hold on to that laughter.

Do you laugh often enough? Maybe you can introduce some more laughter starting from today? Create some fun, read a funny book, listen to some jokes, it's not that hard and it won't take you long.

How do you start your day? Maybe just try starting a little differently, with purpose, and see what changes you experience.

Expect the unexpected

"What time is Lola arriving?" said Nana.

"Anytime soon," said mum.

Lola is coming with us to America, she decided that she might as well help us move. She's good at that, and she thought it would be fun to have a little holiday. Maybe mum's intuition is not too bad after all, the card reading she did for Lola mentioned a trip to America and this bit was coming true! Maybe she will have a whirlwind romance too. How exciting, I couldn't wait for the next chapter in our lives to begin.

"Louie, I think I wrote a poem last night. Did I dream that, or did I just write it in my half-awake state as I was nodding off to sleep?" She did indeed write a poem, it was called, The Dream Catcher. I'll share it with you later on. She was embracing her creative side and it was wonderful to see.

Not long after, I could hear car tyres on the gravel coming up the long winding drive. I could smell Lola's perfume. Did you know, us earth angels have around 278 million sensory receptors compared to your five million, so we can smell things that you can't. Now you know why I can't wait to bathe in the brook after having the deodorant on from my groomer. It's even worse on our noses when humans are making spicy food!

As Lola came to a stop and opened the door, I leapt up into her lap greeting her with a wash.

"Gosh Louie, you have missed me."

Eventually I let Lola get out of the car. I have so much gratitude for this wonderful earth angel, she has been so kind to us.

Nana dished up and we all sat down to brunch. The conversation ensued.

"Are you ready for your holiday, Lola?" asked Gramps.

"I really can't wait. A change of scenery will be most welcomed and I'm looking forward to helping Ellen settle in. That's what friends are for right?"

Mum glanced at Lola with such an appreciative look. Lola would never truly know how much mum valued her. Funny how humans can see immense value in others yet hold back on seeing it in themselves. Mum was starting to see her value now though. I hope you are too?

On the right path

On our way to the airport mum glanced across gramps' shoulder and noticed the fuel was down to 88 miles. "The angels are with us." stated mum. We're definitely doing the right thing Lola. Yes! She's really noticing now.

For you curious lot, you can always google the spiritual meaning of numbers or birds or animals that come into your conscious awareness, but in this instance, I'll tell you. Number 88 relates to progress and success in the future ahead. Are you as excited as I am to find out what happens next? I hope you anticipate the happiness of the future in advance as opposed to worrying about it?

I enjoyed watching mum's journey evolve, not just her outside world and life, but her inner world, intuition and confidence. She was now more trusting and confident in saying yes to opportunities as opposed to her 'Little Miss Worry Pants' identity, who would worry about everything, which thankfully we see less of now. Do you have a version of 'Little Miss Worry Pants'? Or is it something else like 'Little Miss Procrastination Pants' or 'Little Miss Angry Pants'? If you do, please don't value that opinion, it doesn't serve you. Just look at the change in mum when she reduced the volume on 'Little Miss Worry Pants' and turned up the volume on her inner guidance and true self. She has more energy, clarity and happiness. The change on the inside has created opportunities on the outside. Mind blowingly simple, yet not much embraced up until now.

Up, up and away

At the airport, mum and Lola got their suitcases out of the boot of the car. My crate was folded down and they had to assemble it before I could be checked in for my flight. It's very safe for us earth angels to fly, we have a space in an ambient temperature, similar to you humans. It's not the most pleasurable of experiences but needs' must and I get to go to America with mum, so I'm choosing to feel excited.

My favourite humans escorted me to the air freight terminal to check me in. My wishes had come true. All that time ago I was hoping I could go to America with mum and here we are. Not quite the holiday scenario but a relocation is how it manifested.

I said my farewell to Nana and Gramps (for now), and hoped they would come and visit once we had settled in. Nana was crying, mum was crying, both worrying if I would be okay. Of course, I would, we are resilient us earth angels. After a tearful goodbye, I settled down for my flight ahead. Finally, I had some me time and could switch off from my coaching duties.

Several hours later we were on board, I could smell mum's scent so I knew she was close, I hoped she was okay too. At least she has Lola to look after her in my absence.

As we came into land, I braced myself which was unnecessary. What a great captain, it was a nice smooth landing. I thanked my fellow angels for a pleasant flight and the weather angels for not presenting too much turbulence as the doors were opened and daylight shone in. Jeez, that's warm. You know that feeling when you step off a plane and the warm air hits you. Well, that was what I was experiencing. At least you can take your jumpers and coats off, sadly I don't have that option.

Reunited again

When mum was allowed to collect me, she burst into tears with gratitude. I hope 'Little Miss Worry Pants' hadn't been chattering to her all the way to California, now that would've been a long journey.

"Louie, you're okay! I hope that your flight was as comfortable as ours. You'll never guess what happened?" asked mum.

No sign of worry, this is good I thought. Go on then, don't keep me in suspense, share your news.

I can't believe it, we got upgraded, Louie. Just because we took the time to chat to the crew and listen to their problems."

"I think you'll make a great coach, Ellen. You're a natural with people and you really helped them. You deserved to get upgraded, you're so selfless." said Lola.

"You know, you're right, I never felt deserving before because I used to confuse it with greed - but it's okay to have things. I'm slowly learning."

I'm not surprised you got upgraded, mum. After all, there was a fancy looking plane seat on your revised vision board. I observed two of my favourite humans having a conversation and actually receiving compliments from each other. Mum was never good at receiving compliments and feeling deserving or even able to recognise her own superhero qualities that only she possesses or how wonderful she is.

Are you good at receiving compliments and do you recognise your own unique superhero qualities?

Cruising in California

It was time to get our hire car. Mum had booked a bog standard car but when we went to pay and collect our keys, the nice lady offered us a special upgrade price to a convertible. In the high of the moment and after being upgraded on the flight, mum was firmly in yes mode. Saying yes to all opportunities. 'Little Miss Worry Pants' and the accountant in mum was nowhere to be seen, and she didn't worry about paying out an extra bit of money. It was so refreshing to see. Mum was actually living in the present and enjoying life more than ever, no longer saving for a rainy day. Her savings were stacked high enough but Worry Pants was always greedy and always wanted more security. Sometimes it's about balance, and I loved that mum was bringing some back into her life. More fun, and her sparkly personality was starting to shine.

Do you have the right balance in your life? Balance is different for everyone, but be sure to invite balance into your life.

As we stepped outside and walked to the parking lot where our hire vehicle was parked. Mum clicked the key and the 'beep beep' came from the left. As I looked over, it was a red Ford Mustang convertible. Mum and Lola in their excitement loaded the car and immediately put the roof down. I don't think it clicked that it was almost identical to the picture on her vision board. I was not surprised at all. When you really get back into flow and connect with your true inner energy, miracles and dreams can really start coming to life in the most peculiar and swiftest of ways. If you don't believe me, try it. What have you got to lose? Vision, feelings and actions are what create results. Have a vision, connect with how it will make you feel and then show up. Show up every day expecting it to happen, test drive your dream car, bring it into your present consciousness and wait and see what happens. Mum did this with the podcast, she had a vision, she got excited and passionate about helping others and then she said yes to recording the podcast. Dreams do come true!

I was firmly strapped into the back seat, and yes, the seatbelt bra had come with us! I just hope that the brakes on this are better than mum's Ford back home. Funny how there is a theme with Fords. Shame she can't get sponsorship! We set off, the wind in my ears with the Californian breeze brushing past my nose, ears flapping. I notice my reflection in the wing mirror and chuckle to myself that I look like Dumbo, and mum and Lola look like Thelma and Louise. I just hope that she doesn't drive off a cliff and leave you all on a cliff hanger…See what I did there, funny aren't I? I sometimes even laugh at my own jokes. Please laugh at my Spaniel earth angel humour, even if it was a bit of a dad joke. Remember, laughing is good for you.

We were driving on the freeway from San Diego to Carlsbad, following the instruction on the navigation system after mum had merrily put in the zip code and her faith. Ironic, I thought to myself that humans often trust that little piece of electronic kit for physical car journeys, yet seldom trust the journey of life. Do you even put a zip or postcode in for your life and then drive, trusting the journey? Do you need to add a new zip or postcode now?

As mum turned the radio on, it was Dolly Parton '9 to 5', well if this doesn't get you singing along then I don't know what will. Lola and mum started singing their hearts out. Life was good and it's the little moments that are there to be embraced along the journey.

At the end of the song, Lola turned to mum having rephrased some of the lyrics and sang, "you waited for the day for your ship to come in and it's all rolling your way now."

Mum smiled, knowing that all her inner work was paying off. Mum was no longer leaving her life to chance, she was focused on her dreams, and her thoughts matched these, beliefs backing them up and now her ship was rolling in. It takes conscious thought, soul searching and action but your dreams matter and they're more attainable than you think. Are you committing to the inner work?

A different viewpoint

As we arrived in Carlsbad, mum's new boss, Alan, was there to greet us. They had arranged temporary accommodation for mum until she got settled. The apartment overlooked the sea, it was very different to Wales but it was nice to be back by a sea breeze. We had a backyard too with a BBQ area and outdoor seating. I was getting the feeling that we might be able to enjoy some more outdoor living. A stark contrast to the snowballs and winter spas. For now, winter would be a more temperate climate.

Alan had kindly added some staples to the fridge from the local Trader Joe's supermarket and once he knew we were okay, he made his excuses and left, letting mum know to call him if she needed anything.

After getting all the luggage in, we had what we needed for now. Our other homely bits would arrive later. Lola opened the fridge and smiled. "Fancy a glass of wine? I think Alan knows you well, already!" she stated.

Mum didn't need a split second to think about this and as they retreated to the outdoor living area, they sat watching the view over the sea. Tired after a long journey, they were starting to wind down.

"This is it. This is our new life for now. Funny how life has twists and turns, just like a rollercoaster. I'm learning to buckle up and enjoy the ride. I can't believe I'm so calm and excited about all this change, it almost feels like a dream that I'm going to wake up from. Maybe I'm just jet lagged and the panic hasn't set in yet?" mum said to Lola.

Or, maybe you have discovered that you no longer need to try and control everything, that life is constantly flowing and it's there to embrace. Mum was definitely looking at life through a different lens now, seeing things from a different viewpoint. The rainbow tinted lens was more present than the dark lens these days and it was so refreshing to see.

From fear into flow

Several days later after familiarising ourselves with the area, dog friendly parks and outdoor seating spaces, we met up with Lola's cousin, John. Mum was excited to meet him in person after recording the podcast remotely. We met at the Coyote bar and grill. Thankfully, there were no actual Coyotes there. As much as I can control my inner dialogue, I'd prefer not to meet a Coyote face-to-face. John arrived with his friend Scott and I saw Lola blush as he approached the table. Mum was too excited to notice Lola's reaction but I had clocked it. Maybe there was a little attraction with Scott.

The fire pit in the middle of the stone table was lit and even though it was California and May, apparently it was cold for them! To celebrate finally meeting in person, they ordered cocktails. A live band was playing at the far side of the outdoor seating area. Life seems much more in flow these days. What you go looking for, you find and there is always plenty to be grateful for, all around us.

Laughter ensued around the fire pit, food was ordered and consumed, and I even got to share some leftovers.

Lola and Scott were lost in conversation and there was definitely a connection. Scott was easier to talk to than Clive. Remember him. I'm sure most of you have had equally amusing experiences. Well, this was much more pleasant and sophisticated. If nothing else, it may have given Lola hope that it was still possible to find love.

As the afternoon developed, mum had excitedly agreed to co-host Alternative Health Tools on a more permanent basis. She felt honoured to be asked and her dreams were really coming true.

It was time to part company for now and we walked back to our accommodation.

"What a wonderful afternoon," mum beamed. She was truly happy. "What were you talking to Scott about, you two seemed to get on very well?

"Yes, we did," Lola smiled, "He was very pleasant to talk to."

"Ha, maybe my card reading wasn't too far off the mark?" mum joked.

"Let's not get too excited, we live 12 hours apart," said Lola.

"Or, let's just enjoy the moment we have now and let the future take care of itself?" said mum.

I stopped in my tracks. Did mum really just say that? What a profound statement. I am one proud earth angel. Maybe I can semi-retire now. Retiring to California isn't too much of a drag after a winter retreat in Wales.

"How are you feeling about relationships now, Ellen? Do you think you have gotten over Jim yet?"

"Interesting you ask, I was just thinking about that earlier. I think I was fearful of being alone before, but on reflection, I was only in the relationship because I was scared. It was never right. I'm much happier single and I know when the time is right, the relationship angels will present Mr. Right for me. I'm sure of it."

That's my mum. She's learned how to fall in love with herself, enjoy her own company and not be scared of being alone. Have you learned how to fall in love with yourself? Do you enjoy your own company? Whether you are in or out of a relationship, you're always in a relationship with yourself so you might as well make it a good one. After all, you can't dump yourself! Just saying…

Back at the apartment mum and Lola sat in the yard, watching the waves roll in. Lola was asking mum how she felt about her introductory day at the office on Monday. She was having a day to meet the team and had to present some of her ideas on how she could train and coach the team through this transition.

Mum went on to explain that she was feeling a little nervous but she was turning this into excitement, realising that this was her wish and that there was only one thing she could control, and that was her thoughts and how she approached this opportunity. She was going to step up, out of her comfort zone, because after all, this is where life begins, stepping out of fear and into flow. This was more evidence that mum was changing from the inside out, and that the outside was following suit. Don't try and fix everything externally to make you happy. Do it the easier way, start from the inside and watch the outside domino into place.

New acquaintances

It was Monday and Lola had been invited to spend the day with Scott. He was going to show us around whilst mum was settling into her first day at work. Mum left for the office and today she had a different energy about her. Definitely a newfound inner confidence and excitement with a spring in her step. As Lola and I waved her off, wishing her luck, she beamed from ear to ear as she drove off in the red convertible. I must say it suited her, not just the car but the smile too. Don't you find that? People always come to life when they are smiling, properly through their eyes and not just a forced smile like they're posing for a holiday picture.

About an hour later, Scott arrived to collect us. I could hardly believe my eyes. I had to do a double take. For a minute I thought it was Bella hanging out of the back window but no, this was my new acquaintance for today. I was introduced to Porsche, my American Beagle earth angel. Who would've thought I'd have been lucky enough to have two Beagle friends on either side of the pond? I can't wait for Lola to tell Bella. I hope she's not too upset that her mum is away. I'm sure she is having fun at her summer retreat with her grandparents.

Porsche and I sat in the back of the car, Lola and Scott in the front. It was such an eventful day; we visited a dog park in the morning before we stopped off at a seaside café for lunch. It was such an easy day, with great company and Lola was also in flow. It was such a shame she had to return to the UK, for now. Who knows what the future holds, but she was definitely holding on to mum's profound sentiment from the other day and living in the now. That afternoon we were lucky enough to find a dog friendly section of a beach so I could paddle with Porsche, what a perfect day. I hope mum was making some new acquaintances too.

As we returned home, Lola invited Scott to sit with us in the yard. It wasn't long before we heard mum arrive home. She bounced into the yard with the same smile she had been wearing from the morning, she was a completely different person to how she used to arrive home from work in the UK.

"Wow, you look happy," said Lola, "Good day?"

"Yes, it was! I became acquainted with some really nice people, and they were very welcoming. Most of the day was spent familiarising with the accounts, which is still as exciting as it was in the UK, but I decided to approach it with a fresh view. I just feel such huge gratitude for the opportunity."

Mum was realising that whilst we had moved to California and the environment had changed, the day job was still similar. But she was seeing how she could view it differently with rainbow tinted lenses. She got to experience living abroad, meeting new people and even stepping into a blended role where she was now able to help people as well.

"Did you get to present your ideas on how you can train people?" asked Lola.

"Yes, I did, and this is what really excites me, they welcomed a fresh pair of eyes and even noticed I had boundless energy for a Monday when most others were experiencing the Monday morning blues."

Mum never had boundless energy on a Monday before, this was truly different. You could say that it's all new and exciting, and possibly could wear off, but I could see the true change in her. This was here to stay. She definitely had a fresh perspective on life and work.

"Come on Porsche, come and meet Ellen." said Lola, trying to extract Porsche from under the table.

"Oh, my goodness, we have company and not just Scott!" said mum, "Who is this beautiful girl? Louie, she looks just like Bella, you have an American Beagle friend too, how exciting!"

We all sat in the yard, humans chattering away. I knew that when Lola returned home mum would be just fine, her confidence was allowing her to meet new people and also be okay with being alone. Alone is completely different to being lonely.

Imagine, believe and receive

Later that week, mum and Lola were making the most of their final days together before Lola had to return back to the UK. Not forgetting that it was still May, and that Mike Dooley was running an event at a nearby location - well you guessed it - mum only went and got a ticket, another thing on her vision board. She definitely had the hang of this 'imagine, believe and receive'. I think she had finally passed her test, no more 'L' plates required for the vision board.

Lola offered to look after me for the day so mum could attend the event with her work colleague. With mum's new found confidence and independence, I no longer needed to escort her to these events. Maybe Lola was secretly looking forward to spending some extra time with Scott. Love was definitely in the air! It also meant that I got to hang out with Porsche again, and she was fast becoming a good friend.

As mum returned home that evening, she exclaimed, "You won't believe it!"

We probably will, anything is possible when you are in flow.

"I had the pleasure of interviewing Mike Dooley for the 'Alternative Health Tools' podcast, my first live interview."

Seriously mum, only you! Definitely, 'imagine, believe and receive'. I was full of joy and love for this wonderful unique human, she was starting to see how much confidence she had, and a bigger purpose to help others. No longer about her and how her voice sounded on the podcast, it was about giving hope and tools to others around the globe. It's easier to step outside your comfort zone when you have why-power instead of will-power. What's your why-power to get moving in the direction of your dreams?

Chrysalis effect

Two days later we were at home, alone for the first time in Carlsbad. Lola had returned to the UK safely and had been re-united with Bella.

We were back to just the two of us, three if you counted E and probably a whole lot more with the unemployed angels. Ah well, everyone is welcome in our home. So much had happened. However, the biggest shift with mum was her internal state. She was happy, content and peaceful. It's like she was complete, whole and needed nothing or no one to complete her.

A complete metamorphosis from the day the brake line went on the motorway. She had truly experienced the Chrysalis effect. Growing and changing over time into something even more beautiful. The person she was born to be. Shedding the layers that no longer served her; thoughts, beliefs and opinions of others on how she should live her life and what she should expect. The unique human whose birth right was to shine, be happy and fulfilled. External things don't provide this long term if the internal state is not harmonised.

Caterpillars are primed to become butterflies, spreading their wings and showing the world their beauty. What is your beauty and are you really spreading your wings? Have you completely metamorphosed? Metamorphosis for the most part, is a journey and mum is still on this journey. It's not a fixed or immovable destination, it takes time and patience and why-power.

I invite you to shed unwanted thoughts, beliefs and indeed the opinions of others. This is your life and you deserve happiness. Wherever you are on your journey, keep going, we believe in you and want to see you truly shine. Have no regrets. Learn to enjoy where you are right now, because soon, when your dreams continue to unfold, you will want to turn the clock back and replace worry with contentment.

LORD LOUIE'S LESSONS

1. How do you start your morning, is it scatty and straight out, and on the go, or do you take time to centre and ground yourself and design your day?
2. Can you laugh more? What makes you laugh, properly laugh?
3. Do you recognise your own unique superhero qualities?
4. Have you learned to fall in love with yourself? It's the most important relationship that you will have and the only one that will be with you all of your life, so you might as well make the most of it.
5. What thoughts, beliefs and opinions can you unshed to truly shine your light bright to those around you and onto your dreams?

The Journey

Take a step and try
For life is not a race
Tip toe if you must
The journey just embrace

It's your turn to grow
From who you think you are
For when you start the journey
You'll be amazed and will go far

Outside your comfort zone
I invite you to just be
Once you take a little step
The next step you'll just see

Obvious to you
Once you're in the flow
Heart voice cheering for you
Ready, Steady, Go

Life is an adventure
Laughter, fun and happiness
Your birth right to experience
Please expect nothing less

For you deserve to know
That this is how it should be
A world awaits you
Full of opportunity

Start your journey today
Start creating your dream
The universe now working
On gathering up your team

Keep it simple and focus
On what you want to feel
Know that you can make
Anything become real

Embrace the journey dear one
It's the best part of the ride
Twists and turns may come
You no longer need to hide

In the journey you can trust
Just surrender and let it be
Of all that you can dream
Join me, wait, and you'll see

Wherever you start in your journey
Just know that it's okay
Just take a step and trust
Rome wasn't built in a day

Until Next Time

Dear Reader,
Wow! What a journey we have been on since mum gave me my assignment of writing a book and becoming a storyteller. At first, I didn't know what to think. But I stood up to the challenge. I spent many a day observing humans.

My conclusion is that your life is precious and you deserve happiness in whatever form that looks like for you.

I hope you've laughed. I hope you've cried (in a nice way). Tears of joy, tears of breakthrough and tears of release. But most importantly, I hope you have metamorphosed and discovered more about who you are and what you truly want to do with your precious gift of life.

Is there a pot of gold at the end of the rainbow? I personally have never gotten close enough to be able to check. However, you all have a pot of gold inside you. Stop chasing externally for something magical and extraordinary that is already within you. A real treasure chest of feelings, gifts and talents.

A rainbow doesn't need anything to shine. Its colourful beams of light present magic to the people observing it. Move through life like a rainbow, spreading joy and light to those you encounter. Be still in the moment when you want to be, and move in the moment when you want to move.

Stop chasing the rainbow and just be happy now.

With huge universal love,
Yours,
Lord Louie
Lisa Victoria
The angels & the universe
P.S. The Dream Catcher Poem as promised...

Dream Catcher

Shoot for the stars
Dreams abound
For that is where
Magic is found

True magic is not
Just a fairy tale
But something to stir
Wind in the sail

Until you try
To realise your dream
On the hamster wheel
Is how life will seem

Maybe it is lack
Of time, skills or money
That make dreams seem
So distant and funny

It's easy for them
Make time, they say
Clearly, they have
More hours in the day

On they carry
Winning at life
Can't possibly know
My struggle and strife

But they too have family
Commitments and ties
What if my excuses
Are all but lies

Through fear of failure
Territory unknown
Some of my dreams
Have already flown

It's your time now
Just take a step
For your future
Just start to prep

Do what you can
An hour or a minute
To work on your dreams
For a lifetime infinite

With wonderful feelings
Of success and joy
To know you can conquer
Feelings of coy

You can do it
I believe in you
A unique gift to offer
You have that too

Don't let fear
Get in the way
Procrastination for you
Is not okay

Set sail in your boat
Across waters in heat
Naysayers and obstacles
You can beat

Sit and write
What is your gift
Down on paper
To give you a lift

Your heart will guide you
Which thoughts to nourish
In order to allow
You to excel and flourish

Just write without thinking
What comes to mind?
Dreams on the paper
No more searching to find

Magic in the sails
Excitement in the air
Robes of dreams
You're now able to wear

Take action daily
Watch the seeds grow
For your life and your purpose
Are now back in flow

Shine your colour bright
It's your time and your place
The rainbow is you
Not something to chase

Please don't stop here on your journey. We'd love for it to continue, to share it with you, and to hear your insights and breakthroughs over in our like 'hearted' Facebook community. Here is the link to join our Facebook group (Lead with the Heart - https://www.facebook.com/groups/leadwiththeheart)

If you haven't done so already, don't forget to download your complimentary workbook with Lord Louie's questions from the end of each chapter, to support your own self-discovery. There really is huge value in writing things down instead of just 'thinking' them through.

You can get your workbook here:
heartvoice.co.uk/behappynow

References

Broadband Consciousness – Richard Wilkins & Elizabeth Ivory www.theministryofinspiration.com

Mike Dooley – Notes from the universe. www.tut.com

Lorna Byrne www.lornabyrne.com

It's a Wonderful Life, 1946 film https://en.wikipedia.org/wiki/It%27s_a_Wonderful_Life

Katy Perry – Roar https://www.youtube.com/watch?v=CevxZvSJLk8

Electric Light Orchestra - Hold on Tight https://www.youtube.com/watch?v=UkekqVPIc2M

Yazz – The only way is up https://www.youtube.com/watch?v=vjD3EVC1-zU

Dolly Parton – 9 to 5 https://www.youtube.com/watch?v=UbxUSsFXYo4

Alternative Health Tools podcast https://www.alternativehealthtools.com/085-mike-dooley-law-of-attraction-thoughts-become-things/

Printed in Great Britain
by Amazon